Iconic Cycling Trails in Wales

Phil Horsley

SWANSEA LIBRARIES

6000307688

Gwasg Carreg Gwalch

First published in 2017
© text: Phil Horsley
© images: Gwasg Carreg Gwalch and Crown copyright (2016) Visit Wales; Pierino Algieri: pages 12, 82, 83, 87, 96, 98, 109, 110.
© publication: Gwasg Carreg Gwalch 2017

All rights reserved. No part of this publication may be reproduced, stored in a retrieval system, or transmitted in any form or by any means, electronic, electrostatic, magnetic tape, mechanical, photocopying, recording, or otherwise, without prior permission of the authors of the works herein.

ISBN: 978-1-84524-263-3
Cover design: Eleri Owen; Map: Alison Davies

Published by Gwasg Carreg Gwalch,
12 Iard yr Orsaf, Llanrwst, Wales LL26 0EH
tel: 01492 642031
email: llyfrau@carreg-gwalch.com
website: www.carreg-gwalch.com

Disclaimer

While every effort has been made to check the veracity of all the information in this book, mistakes can happen. I am human. If you should discover an error, I apologise.

Llwybr Mawddach Trail

Contents

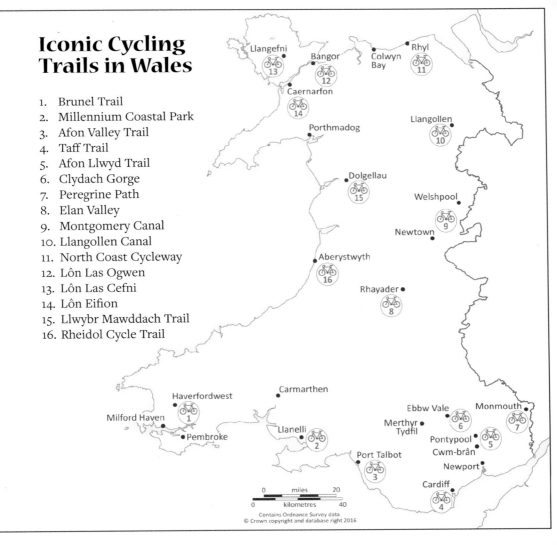

Iconic Cycling Trails in Wales

1. Brunel Trail
2. Millennium Coastal Park
3. Afon Valley Trail
4. Taff Trail
5. Afon Llwyd Trail
6. Clydach Gorge
7. Peregrine Path
8. Elan Valley
9. Montgomery Canal
10. Llangollen Canal
11. North Coast Cycleway
12. Lôn Las Ogwen
13. Lôn Las Cefni
14. Lôn Eifion
15. Llwybr Mawddach Trail
16. Rheidol Cycle Trail

Contains Ordnance Survey data
© Crown copyright and database right 2016

Introduction

'Surely by its silence, its simplicity, its efficiency, and its economy the bicycle is the most divine invention of contemporary man. Every doctor should be a cyclist.'

S. L. Henderson Smith M.D.

These cycle trails count among the best in Britain, quite possibly the world, for where else can you cycle traffic-free from golden beaches to high rocky mountains in a few short miles; past medieval strongholds, through dappled woodland, along tidal estuaries, and over, under, across and around structures and buildings of true class and innovation.

These are family friendly cycle routes and can be ridden safely by even the most inexperienced cyclist, but they can be enjoyed by all ages and abilities, including the mature cyclist who climbs Mont Ventoux only in their dreams. Some are more demanding than others, and for the intrepid the routes can be extended or adapted instead of backtracking.

For these trails we must thank the workers and their families of the Industrial Revolution, for laying the tramways and railways and digging the canals and building the waterfronts on which they run. Also today's planners and elected representatives in recognising their potential. If we are to have a safe, life enhancing, sustainable future then cycling must be a key component, and all cyclists start young.

It matters, of course, that the trails are in Wales. Some of the trails are in the Welsh-speaking heartland (Penygroes is 88% Welsh-speaking), and there is some amused affection at the nonconformity of the language in different parts of the country (and a shared exasperation at official Welsh), but you must remember that Cymru means 'compatriots', the only country in the world where the land is named after the people sharing it.

The sixteen Trails described here reflect the glorious spectrum of cycling available in Wales. You may not have the irrepressible enthusiasm of Annie to lead the way, but you'll meet all manner of fascinating folk on a bike, most of whom

Cycling along the Brecknock and Abergavenny Canal path

are happy to share a little time. I've come across royalty, Australians, dentists and anarchists. I met a cyclist with a broken-winged pigeon on his handlebars, and another with an inhabited dog kennel over his panniers. Here you'll find the natural world at its very best; mighty dams and spider-legged piers; and rock worn, weathered and blasted from the innards of the earth. Here you'll find candy floss and tea.

> *'The cyclist can be keenly aware of the future. He sees, smells, hears, feels and even tastes changes in the environment through which he cycles.'*
>
> *Michael H. Farny*

This book is about the joy of cycling, the space it frees in your mind, the release of emotional well-being, the physical pleasure of your working body, the opportunity cycling provides to open up a view of the world.

Enjoying cycling in every corner of Wales: 1. Bryn Bach, Tredegar; 2. Llynnau Cregennan, nr Dolgellau; 3. Cwm Tydu, Ceredigion

> *'I don't ride my bike all over the place because it is ecological or worthy. I mainly do it for the sense of freedom and exhilaration.'*
>
> *David Byrne*

The bicycle takes you from the world of virtual reality into the real world and in the process it forces your body to work. For a while it gives you power. You are in control.

> *'In a sedentary and alienating age, cycling is one of the ideal recreations– a simple, refreshing way of seeing the world.'*
>
> *Richard Ballantine*

In every Yorkshire kitchen-sink drama there is a moment when Dad (braces, short back and sides, carpet slippers) asks the rebellious son/daughter, "Aye, but what's it all for?" Slavoj Zizek in the film 'A Perverts Guide to Ideology' pushes us forward. The future, he says, depends on your dreams, and the first step is to free your dreams

'The action of the imagination brings home to the bicycle-rider the limitlessness of the potential in all things.'

William Saroyan

At night, with the moon hidden and the solar system alight you may notice in the constellation in the northern sky, first spotted by the Pole, Bruno Schulz, of a cyclist, centred upon Corona Borealis.

To bring us back down to Earth, I give you the following benefits of cycling:

– There is an inverse dose-response relationship to your overall health from all physical activity, i.e. as the level of physical activity rises, the risk of all-cause mortality falls. In other words, after quitting smoking, exercise is the best way for you to keep healthy.
– Studies show that cycling to work cuts your risk of dying by 30% to 40%.
– People who have a physically inactive lifestyle have double the risk of a heart attack.
– Physical inactivity can increase the risk of developing Type 2 diabetes by 33% to 50%.
– Studies have indicated an inverse, dose-response relationship between physical activity and cancer.
– Inactive people are more likely to develop clinically defined depression.
– Physical activity has a particularly positive effect on osteoporosis, osteoarthritis and lower back pain.
– Improved physical activity helps older people with strength, balance, co-ordination, flexibility and reaction.
– Various studies have shown that cycling has the greatest effect on fitness of all physical activities due to the more even distribution of impact on your bone structure, plus the rhythm of cycling enables you to undertake more physical activity at any one time than any other form of exercise.
– Cycling burns on average around five kilocaleries per minute.
– A large study in Denmark showed that 'those who did not cycle to work experience a 39% higher mortality rate than those who did'.

1. Brecknock and Abergavenny Canal Path; 2. Elan Valley; 3. Tenby

– 24,000 people die prematurely in Britain per annum from exposure to air pollution from road traffic.

– Figures for death and injury to cyclists in the UK as a whole are falling. Statistically the actual risk is one cycling death per 33 million kilometres of cycling. It would take an average cyclist 21,000 years to cycle this distance. In 2011 there were 96 cyclists killed on Britain's roads. In the same year 655 people died falling down stairs, and 1,523 deaths were caused by accidental poisoning. You are 9 times more likely to be killed in a car than on a bike.

The movement of a person on a human-powered machine is perhaps the most perfect way of enabling our minds to comprehend and appreciate the living world. It is no co-incidence that most of these trails are upon the remaining debris of a once mighty industrial complex. We are in transition from a dehumanising and oppressive industrial society to something else, though exactly what is not yet clear. Cycling encourages a clarity of thought lost in the madness of today's traffic.

Every year the whole city of Brussels has a car-free day. It is safe to cycle everywhere. Last time I was there we were overtaken by King Philippe and Queen Mathilde, to cries of "Allez, allez, Philippe". Cardiff had its first, very limited, car-free day in September 2016. You do not have to wait for the one day a year to come around. All these iconic cycle routes are available all year, every year. Improve your mind, improve your health, improve the planet. What are you waiting for?

Lôn Las Ogwen in the heart of the Snowdonia mountains

1. Brunel Trail / Llwybr Brunel

Neyland to Haverfordwest

Distance: *16 km / 10 m*
OS Map: *1:50,000*
157 St David's and
Haverfordwest
Leaflet: *Sustrans Brunel Trail*
Access and Parking:
Brunel Quay, Neyland
Upper Crossing Cottage,
Rosemarket
Johnston
Haverfordwest
Pembroke Dock (cycle paths over
the Cleddau Bridge)
Surface: *Tarmac*
Nearby places of interest:
Pembroke Dock Heritage Centre,
The Royal Dockyard
(www.sunderlandtrust.org.uk)
West Wales Maritime Heritage
Society, Front Street,
Pembroke Dock
Haverfordwest Town Museum,
The Castle.

The Brunel Trail is signed '4 Celtic Trail / Lôn Geltaidd' in a rather undemonstrative fashion, and disconcertingly NOT 'Brunel Trail'. The Celtic Trail is a Sustrans route covering 220 miles from Fishguard to Chepstow.

Begin at the statue of I. K. Brunel at Neyland Quay, with its information boards (in need of a little TLC) and fine cyclorama including Pembroke Dock and Milford Haven. The Trail gently ascends from the riverside corridor of Westfield Pill through quiet woodland to Johnston, where it is joined by the active railway from Milford. The blissful intimate feeling is maintained as the Trail wanders a little and undulates slightly, passing a corrugation of Nissan huts and a congregation of uplifted wild trees reaching for the light. Fellow cyclists are riding everything from carbon-framed, through customised and souped-up to folding and vintage (some verging on jalopy) and vary from excitable family

The Brunel statue at Neyland

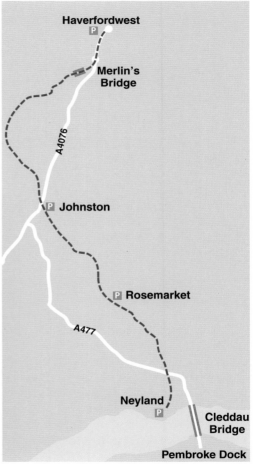

groups to the glammed-up and powerfully stomach'd.

The allure is diminished somewhat upon reaching Macdonalds at the Merlin's Bridge roundabout near Haverfordwest, where the Trail is accompanied for the next mile or so by the thundering H'West bypass, and ends haphazardly among the commercial bustle of the town. Locals park on the roadside near the Golden Arches.

I. K. Brunel

In 2002 Isambard Kingdom Brunel was voted the Second Greatest Briton Of All Time, after Laura Trott, or perhaps it was Churchill. He was one of the Nineteenth Century engineering giants.

The names are from the families of his parents, but he was born in a modest terraced house. His dad, a Frenchman called Marc Isambard Brunel, made a fortune equipping the British army with ill-fitting boots, lost it all when peace erupted after the Battle of Waterloo and ended up in debtors prison. His wife, of course, accompanied him into prison to darn his socks, and young I. K. was sent to boarding school to hone his engineering skills, then college in Paris, followed by a clock-maker's apprenticeship. He went back to London to work in his father's engineering office, when they won the contract to dig the Rotherhythe-Limehouse Tunnel. At the time this was thought impossible due to underground quicksand and the mighty river not far above their heads. I. K. assumed full control of the project aged 21 and more or less lived on the job. When bits of china and old boots fell into the tunnel, from the bottom of the river above, he used an open bottom diving bell to inspect the river bed, wearing swimming trunks. Another time he was rescued unconscious from a wave of floodwater sweeping through the tunnel. The frequent inundations forced it to be abandoned and bricked up and only many years later was it made watertight and incorporated into the Underground.

This failure forced I. K. to question his abilities, but he was imbued with supreme confidence and his next job was the Clifton Suspension Bridge, also seen as an impossible task. When the start was delayed by a three day riot, Brunel signed on as a special constable. It worked, the bridge was completed, and led to his next job. At the age of 27, in 1833, he was appointed Chief Engineer to a new project, the Great Western Railway. I. K. being I. K., decided everyone else was wrong and the track should be wider, a seven foot gauge. The engine boiler sitting between the wheels would give a smoother, faster and safer ride (less toppling over when cornering). It also meant wider bridges and tunnels, including the one and three quarter mile Box Hill Tunnel (Box Hill these days famed, of course, as the centrepiece of the London Olympic Cycle Road race, won by Kazakhstan's Vinokourov and watched en route by a million people). Possible problems with I.K.'s track width at, say, Birmingham, where the two gauges met, were left to the future. Note; on the Quayside at Neyland sections of the broad gauge rails are used as handrails.

Now he had a career, I. K. went looking for a wife, and was introduced to the talented artistic and musical family, the Horsleys (no relation, but I'm still looking). The father composed 'There is a Green Hill Far Away', but I. K.'s eye was drawn to the gorgeous 19 year old Mary. The honeymoon was short, a couple of nights in Capel Curig, then a dash down to Cheltenham for a GWR progress report. Mary, for her part, played the trophy wife to a T, attending the Opening of Railways bejewelled and in silk gowns, and requiring the attendance of a liveried footman for her strolls around the local London park. Brunel was away on business much of the time, living and working in a horse-drawn carriage known as the 'flying hearse'.

Having reached Bristol, I. K. conceived the notion of the purchasing of a ticket at Paddington Station to New York, although no steamship had yet been built capable of crossing the Atlantic. Brunel took up the challenge and his first ship, P.S.S. Great Western made sixty seven crossings in the next eight years.

When, in 1848, the GWR entered South Wales the problem of the different gauges became a nuisance with, at various interchange stations, a good deal of pushing and shoving as the passengers swapped trains. The problem was resolved simply because there was more standard gauge track than wide (though interestingly, Indian Railways today use a wider track).

Milford Haven (*Aberdaugleddau*) is a ria, a sunken river valley, drowned at the end of the last Ice Age, and one of the deepest natural harbours in the world. A variety of ships use the waterway, including oil tankers and the huge LPG / LNG tankers, so large they require a one mile exclusion zone on the approach. Milford has been a port since the Middle Ages but the town was founded by Sir William Hamilton as a whaling port. The Royal Navy intervened, using it as a dockyard from 1800. Two years later, Vice Admiral Horatio Nelson, at the height of his fame, visited Milford and Haverfordwest on a triumphal business trip, accompanied by Sir William, now in his seventieth year, and his wife Lady Emma Hamilton, 35, and Horatio's lover. The Navy later moved across the water to Pembroke Dock and Milford became an important fishing and commercial harbour, so when Brunel came looking for a port to act as a transatlantic terminus for the GWR he chose the tiny village of Neyland, five miles upriver.

The railway arrived in 1856 and a new town was built for the railway and dock workers. A steamship service began to Ireland, then in 1858 to Portugal and Brazil. A visit by I. K. himself fuelled speculation that Neyland might be chosen as the home port of the giant P.S.S. Great Eastern, then under construction in London. He came again a year later, with Mary, but within twelve months he was dead. Brunel was a heavy smoker.

Neyland

For the next fifty years Neyland bustled with the trade to Ireland. A huge pontoon, 154 feet long, and built with 300 tons of iron and 600 tons of wood was built for the embarkation of people and cattle. The Great Eastern visited in 1860 and 1862. The village boomed to over 1,000, with 4 chapels and a large hotel. BUT-

> The Irish ferry traffic went to Fishguard in 1906.
> The naval dockyard at Pembroke Dock closed in 1926.
> The last train from Haverfordwest ran in 1964.
> The South Wales Hotel was demolished in 1970.

1. Cleddau bridge and Neyland marina;
2. Haverfordwest

The Hobbs Point Ferry closed in 1975 when the Cleddau Bridge opened.

AND YET
The Brunel Festival is held in July.
The Brunel Trail opened soon after the Millennium.

Snippets
Annie
I met Annie near H'West. She was a carver of love-spoons. I know, this is the wrong way round and love-spoons were traditionally carved by the suitor, but that's Annie for you.

2. Millennium Coastal Park / Llwybr Arfordirol y Mileniwm, Llanelli

Bynea to Pembrey

Distance: 16.5 km / 10.5 m

OS Map: 1:50,000
159 Swansea and Gower

Leaflet: Sustrans Millennium Coastal Park

Access and Parking:
Pembrey Country Park
Burry Port
Pwll
Llanelli
Bynea
Access throughout

Surface: Tarmac mostly, with some hardcore and a short rough section near Bynea which floods on the spring tides.

Nearby places of interest:
Kidwelly Castle
Kidwelly Industrial Museum
National Wetlands centre
Discovery Centre, Llanelli
Pembrey Country Park

The Trail is marked with yellow capped poles and also '4', with local destinations. Of course it can be accessed anywhere but both ends are termed Gateways, and whereas Bynea Gateway, off the A484 near Loughor, is clear, the Pembrey Gateway is less so. Route 4 comes in to Burry Port from Kidwelly (*Cydweli*) along an old railway track marked '4 Canal Path', but the actual Gateway lies in the huge open complex of Pembrey Country Park, and follows the Wales Coast Path along a track across Pembrey Burrows, skirting the dunes and overlooking the Saltings. Follow the yellow capped poles. Unless you are a pernickety person, it doesn't really matter if you wander a little for this really is a parallel universe, divorced from past and present hardship and woe. The car parks at Burry Port are labelled 'Park+Bicycle'. The run along the coast is a flat, flowing, popular leg-stretcher with sculptured landscaping, nature reserves, informative plaques and a gamut of space and scenery. Can we have a lot more of these please?

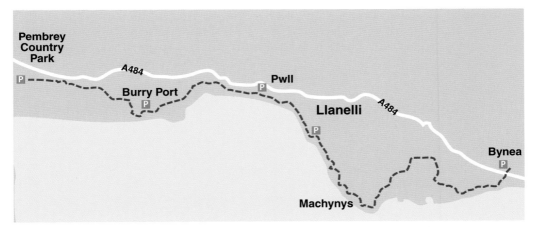

(Oh, did we really vote to leave the EU?) Across the sands and mud-flats is the Gower and between, depending on the tide, are bait diggers and cocklers and who knows what the other folk are doing.

What comes to mind when I mention Llanelli? Jake Ball's beard? Felinfoel Double Dragon? The spare tyre? Indeed the car's spare tyre was invented by Tom and Walter Davies in 1904 in a garage in Stepney Street, and is still known today on the Subcontinent as a 'Stepney'.

The Stepneys, from Stepney in London, married into Pembrokeshire in the C17th, and were indeed great marryers, until.... Sir John, for example, the Fourth Baronet married Justina Mariana, the daughter of the Flemish painter Van Dyck, and Sir Thomas, the Fifth, married into Llanelli, and occupied Llanelly House (which today is 'Llanelli's premier visitor attraction', with renowned kitchen and ghost), Sir Thomas was THE Stepney businessman.

By the time we get to the Eighth, another Sir John, the moral backbone of the Stepneys had slumped. Sir John had a penchant for horse-racing, cards and Society beauties. He never married but spawned an unknown number of illegitimate sons, none of whom gets a mention on his memorial plaque in St Elli Parish Church.

The Ninth, another Sir Thomas, died 'without issue'. It was he who developed the coal trade in the town, plus he acquired a reputation as the father of the poor. His official position in London Society was 'Groom of Bed-Chamber to the Duke of York', a position of household importance exceeded only by the Groom of the Stool. On his death the title to the estates became complicated, with various Aunts marrying a 'loan contractor' whose 'indolence equalled his extravagance'; a General; and a Politician, and the name Stepney became hyphenated in a variety of ways.

I'm teasing of course, what comes immediately to mind is Dyfed Steels, and Llanelli's nickname used to be Tinopolis. Working with steel still goes on: Dyfed Steels folds, punches, shears, grinds and profiles steel; the Trostre works makes tinplate steel for drinks cans and aerosols, and 3K's made the folding roof over Wimbledon's Centre Court, but times have changed and you are cycling through part of Wales's future. Swansea Bay is the title of the new City Region which is the focus for the complex and uncertain future in this globalised world. Swansea Bay, it is hoped, will bring together our two great uncertainties; we'd like to know our place in the world again, our role, what we are here for; and secondly we'd like our politicians to represent us, to be aware of our uncertainties and to think of us when decisions are made.

The Route (from the East)
Bynea Gateway

The start of the Millennium Coastal Park. The Loughor Estuary opens up before you, today an SSSI and Special Area of Conservation. No sign of the copper smelting plant over at Penclawdd, nor the Batteries, though the marshes have been regularly swept for high explosive and mustard gas shells. Sheep graze the reclaimed salt marshes, unaware that their ancestors participated in anthrax biological warfare testing. Consideration is being given to fracking, underwater coal gassification and an upstream barrage.

National Wetland Centre

Noted for a wonderful gathering of wetland birds and dragonflies.

Machynys Peninsula

Gary Nicklaus' golf course was built in the '80s. Nothing remains of the C19th factories, brickworks and chemical plants, or the two communities (though the embankment was built to protect the industry, not the golf course). Sensitive nostrils can detect an aura of oil hanging over the nearby Trostre works.

The North Dock

Home to the Discovery Centre, Water Sports Centre and seaside promenade. In the 1880s an eighth of Britain's tinplate was exported from here, much of it to the USA.

Pwll

The embankment was built by Brunel for rail passengers to Neyland and beyond. The huge Carmarthen Bay Power Station has gone.

Burry Port (*Porth Tywyn*)

The harbour was used to ship coal, and the products from the tinplate, copper, silver and lead works which grew alongside.

Pembrey (*Pen-bre*)

The mountain behind was thoroughly mined and the coal exported from here until silting caused the development of Burry Port harbour. In World War 2 parts of the Ashburnham estate were used as a firing range, which continues on Pembrey Sands, and RAF Pembrey was home to both fighter and bomber aircraft. The airport is still a working airfield as well as the National Motorsports Centre.

Its confession time; every now and then I have an irresistible desire for a Parsons pickled egg. Annie knows not to interfere, and to give me a wide berth afterwards. But Parsons of Burry Port are better known as the only British bottlers of pickled cockles and mussels, and these come from the Burry Inlet, so when, in 2001, the shellfish beds were closed due to diarrhetic poisoning, the Welsh Assembly wanted to know why, especially as conservation was key to local regeneration. (50,000 wildfowl over-winter here.)

Well, gosh, it's complicated, Pollution from humans, past and present, is particularly pertinent in estuarine waters though we are way beyond the 'out of sight, out of mind' era. Metal inputs, iron, copper, zinc etc. mainly from abandoned mines, have declined since the 1980s; sewage treatment has improved since the 1990s; excess nitrogen from farming still flows down the rivers; but nothing specifically explained the 2001 poisoning. Also, they noticed, it was happening simultaneously in the Thames Estuary, the Wash and Strangford Lough. Current thinking is that sudden blooms of toxic marine microalgae are linked to climate change. Between 2013 and 2015 an unprecedented sea warming off the US Pacific coast produced huge toxic blooms of algae, and a horrible death count of fin whales, otters, seals and fish.

When the beds reopened in 2005 there was a stampede of cockle pickers from all over the UK.

Other local cycle trails

The Swiss Valley Cycle Route runs for 11 miles traffic free from Llanelli, past the Felinfoel Brewery to Lleidi Reservoir and Cross Hands. This ride is not flat. A further seven mile link, mixed on / off road will take you to the National Botanic Garden of Wales, with its Great Glass House. Download a map at www.sustrans.org.uk.

Route 4 continues from Bynea Gateway to Gowerton and across the Gower before following the Clyne Valley down to Swansea Bay at Black Pill, then east along the waterfront to Swansea. Much of this is off road. From Llanelli to Swansea is 19 miles / 30 km.

3. Afan Valley Trail / Cwm Afan

Port Talbot to the Afan Forest Park

Distance: *26 km / 14 m*

OS Map: *1:50,000*
170 Vale of Glamorgan

Leaflet: *Information available at the Sustrans website*

Access and Parking:
Port Talbot, Aberavon Beach
Pontrhydyfan
Rhyslyn
Afan Argoed
Cymmer
Glyncorrwg
Blaengwynfi

Surface: *Mostly tarmac*

Nearby places of interest:
Margam Abbey
Margam Abbey Stones Museum
South Wales Miners Museum

'Problems of urban deprivation have their origins in the deviant pathologies of individuals.' This is from a Government report in 1970 announcing the launching of CDPs, Community Development Projects, as a 'neighbourhood based experiment aimed at finding new ways of meeting the needs of people living in areas of high social deprivation.'*

Hang on, this is a book about Cycle trails! As a visiting cyclist you are not riding in a vacuum, but past the back doors of people, and drinking tea in their cafes. Annie fell for the young policeman, especially when he asked to see her passport before entering the valley.

This trail is the Hidden Gem, a passage of peace and contentment slipping through the folds of valleys. As a Cumbrian once told me "Them as knows comes, them as doesn't, doesn't."

The trail has two names. Locally it is known as Y Rheilffordd (*the Railway*), but Sustrans labelled it 887 and began the trail at Aberavon Beach in Port Talbot, although the policemen told Annie, "It's not nice down there". Aberavon Promenade, on a sunny morning, is glorious with the locals out in force. The beach is Blue Flag and the Prom has been refurbished for cyclists to enjoy Franco's Fish and Chips, the steel 'Kite Tail' and the Blue Whale.

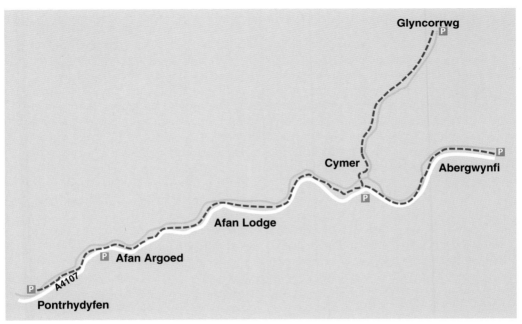

Across the way is the steelworks.

I worked in my student holidays at Lysaghts steelworks in 'Scunny', employed to work alongside the Irish and Scots labourers to clean out and tidy up. What a filthy, dangerous, dynamic place to work. Each shop had a board giving 'Days Since the Last Fatality'. There were always men on the move, jumping the lines of red hot steel, watching the wire being stretched, listening for the warning cry "she's flying", but always, if you could, you made your way to the first rollers where white hot ingots were manoeuvred and squeezed. It never failed to thrill. Making steel is not like that now, the town not covered in red dust, the Irish no longer buying an off the peg suit every other Friday and wearing it to work and drink (and to bed for all I knew).

In the mid 1960s the Abbey Steelworks at Margam employed 20,000. It was the largest steelworks in Europe and the biggest single employer in Wales. Today it employs less than 4,000 and the future is uncertain. Is this how capitalism is supposed to work; a life of grind, spending what you earn, enriching the rich, and spat out when the industry moves away?

Cycle Trail 887 should have been a good idea, but as diversion piled on diversion in Port Talbot it became too much for us and we took to the roads. So, in my humble opinion, you're best starting in the Afan Valley itself, parking in Pontrhydyfan by the church, or at the Rhyslyn car park, or Afan Argoed (the mountain bike centre, all testosterone and mud), although I mustn't put you off, and for the intrepid there is an interactive map for cyclists for the whole of Swansea Bay on *www.cycleswanseabay.org.uk*.

Ride over the viaduct in Pontrhydyfan, built as an aqueduct nearly 200 years ago to carry water to power the blast furnace wheel in John Reynolds ironworks, then just follow the railway; the wind in the trees, rushing water, birdsong; it's lovely. There are plenty of locals on hand, walking dogs, sipping at the Cymmer Station Refreshment Rooms and offering helpful advice. In Cymmer the trail splits.

One valley goes to Glyncorrwg, starting over the Cymmer Arch Bridge, built in 1920 out of reinforced concrete, and at the time one of the largest single span concrete bridges. In the village the mountain bike centre doubles as a mother and baby meeting room. The other valley goes to the twin villages of Blaengwynfi / Abergwynfi with its cafe / bar G2 (and corrugated iron banqueting room) and spaceship primary school.

The apparently simple railway track belies its origin with four railway companies meeting at Cymmer, with lines disappearing into the hillsides in tunnels, which I suppose was par for the course in a valley dominated by coal mines. There is talk, and I'm referring to Annie's constable pal, of re-opening the tunnels for cyclists.

So what does the future hold here? Vattenfall, the MTB centre sponsors, are erecting windmills and nearby plans were submitted for a new private coal mine, but the accepted policy is that the future of the Afan Valley lies in tourism, with a recent proposal for a £55m. Centre Parcs style resort with ski slope and golf course, though local opinion is coloured by the Glyncorrwg Ponds, a 1990s sop to the hardship caused by the closure of the pits. Forgotten mining communities have raw and emotional edges. As Carr and Schöne say 'Attract tourists by all means, but don't try to pretend that mining didn't exist in this valley'. The relationship of Welsh society with its coal mining heritage has been described as 'schizophrenic', with immense pride in the culture surrounding this filthy and dangerous work and an acknowledgement of its historical economic importance. On the other hand it has left immense landscape pollution and a high human cost (including the 144 people killed in Aberfan [Aberfan is in Merthyr Vale, that's three valleys over] in 1966 and the 1913 explosion at Senghenydd near Caerphilly, which killed 439 men and boys.) Nothing of significance has replaced the pits, and just as the Welsh government is accused of dragging its feet in response to the threat posed by climate change, so it has been suggested that the authorities have been too conservative in their approach to these forgotten villages and towns. Oh, you'll just have to read the book.

Coalfaces by Tina Carr and Annemarie Schöne (2008, Llandysul, Gwasg Gomer), subtitled *Life after coal in the Afan Valley*.

Snippet

It was whilst riding these valleys that Annie and I got talking about the pleasures of riding traffic free, and how, someday we will be able to cycle everywhere without worrying about being hit from behind by a car (which happened to my mate Peter some years ago). In the meanwhile, what do we do? We persuaded ourselves that we need to look into folding bicycles in order to utilise public transport for the places that are too dangerous to cycle.

Other local cycle trails

Route 4 continues south east from Port Talbot through Margam Country Park to Bridgend, a mixture of on and off road.

885 continues from Cymer through the other ex coal mining village of Caerau and on to Maesteg, mainly off road.

884 is an off road route from Bryngarw Country Park up to Blaengarw, eight miles long, in part alongside the Daffodil Line, a

section of railway being restored as the Garw Valley Railway.

The Ogmore Valley Trail is another traffic free path from the Bridgend suburb of Aberkenfig up to Nant-y-Moel, another valley transformed from rural hill farming to industry with the opening of coal mines. The last pit closed in 1983.

The RCT Council (Rhondda Cynon Taf) is planning an off road cycle path from Pontypridd up the Rhondda to Blaencwm, where, it is hoped, the tunnel will be reopened through to the Afan Valley for cyclists.

Blaengwynfi

4. Taff Trail / Taith Taf

Cardiff to Castell Coch

Distance: *11 km / 7 m*
OS Map: *1:50,000*
171 Cardiff and Newport
Leaflet: *Sustrans Taff Trail*
Access and Parking:
Cardiff Bay / Atlantic Wharf
Sophia Gardens
Forest Farm
Castell Coch
Access throughout
Surface: *Tarmac*
Nearby places of interest:
Cardiff Bay Millennium
Waterfront
National Museum Cardiff
Cardiff Castle
Llandaff Cathedral
Castell Coch
Museum of Welsh Life, St Fagans

The Taff Trail has iconic status because...well...well...perhaps the Idea is greater than the Being. It is venerable, opened in 1988 by Wyn Roberts, Baron Roberts of Conwy, as a long (55 mile, 89 k.) traffic-free route out of the heart of the city. It also follows the line of the railways and canal which carried the iron and coal which drove the city. That history has almost entirely been swallowed by modern Cardiff, and the Taff Trail suffers as it shoehorns cyclists and pedestrians into the same limited city space.

The signing is '8 Taff Trail' and it begins at the Celtic Ring sculpture in Roald Dahl Plass at the Pierhead, or does it? This is now part of '8 Bay Trail', which circumnavigates Cardiff Bay (approx. 6 km). Ride this clockwise for it is easy to lose it amongst the new developments around International Drive, Empire Way and Olympian Drive, where just about every footpath is shared and there are two enigmatic signs saying, 'End of Cycle Route'. Oh, for a Cosmic Cyclepath.

There are more ambiguous moments in Grangetown until the Millennium Stadium is passed and the embankment is gained at Sophia Gardens. When I say 'ambiguous' I mean motorists doing silly things (it is partly on-road); cyclists doing

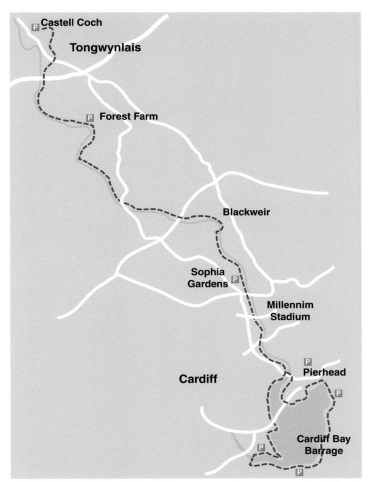

Castell Coch

Tongwynlais

Forest Farm

Blackweir

Sophia
Gardens

Millennim
Stadium

Pierhead

Cardiff

Cardiff Bay
Barrage

silly things ("Oh sorry") and pedestrians walking about staring at smartphones (lost in transition?) or isolated behind earphones (cantabolic?). In the urban jungle people are just different.

Beyond Blackweir the trail swaps banks and the next section through woodland alongside the quietly flowing river is a pleasure to ride, though often liberally sprinkled with D.W.s (dog walkers), runners, pram pushers and fellow cyclists. This is the line of the Glamorganshire Canal and in a while you come across the Melin Gruffydd Water Pump, a water powered beam engine of 1807, built to pump water up to the canal. It worked until 1948 when the canal was filled in.

Forest Farm is a nature reserve with canal sections still in water, and beyond that Radyr Weir has twin Archimedes Screws producing electricity with an annual CO_2 saving of 785 tonnes. The trail takes to the streets of Tongwynlais for a while before a short steep climb up to Castell Coch, or a continuation towards Taff's Well, jostling with the multi-lane highways; an acceptable section of the route, but not a pleasurable one.

20% of all cycling accidents in Wales happen in Cardiff. The Cardiff Cycling Campaign is calling for a 'sea-change' in thinking. When they organised a cycle ride in the city for a group of councillors, the latter described it as 'frightening', and 'an eye opener'. City cycling doesn't have to be a gawky, second-best experience, uncomfortably sharing limited space with pedestrians, or fighting it out on the roads with cars and lorries. Cyclists in cities are replacing cars. Other cities are beginning to realise that separate cycling provision can be achieved by removing space from moving vehicles, and also, crucially, by reducing space for parking.

(You may well be surprised that Annie does not have something to say on the matter. She's not with me. When in Cardiff she slips off to see her favourite Richard Hawley lookalike at Kelly's Records to talk bands and singers. Jesse Colin Young? Anyone?)

My annual visits to Normanton near Wakefield in the 1960s left me with deep scars, but our thrashing (rugby union, prop forward, I was one of the "all shapes

The Taff river and the old dockland area of Cardiff – now the Cardiff Bay

and sizes") at the hands of the bigger, harder, meaner Normanton boys I always put down to their career choices; rugby league or the pit. In 1757 Richard Crawshay had the choice of neither, but he was one of those boys, and at the age of 16, and following a bloody-minded 'do' with his Dad, he set off for London on horseback. There he became known as 'The Yorkshire Boy'. He apprenticed in a bar iron warehouse and worked his way up, marrying the boss's daughter on the way, before buying an interest in Merthyr's Cyfarthfa Ironworks and making cannon, cannonballs and other weaponry (most of the early ironworks made weaponry). When he died Richard was 'the wealthiest of commoners', leaving an estate worth £1½ million. By then he was know as 'The Tyrant'.

Of course Richard Crawshay is one half of the story; poverty, sweat and grinding labour being the other.

He was famous enough to entertain Lord Nelson and Lady Hamilton on their triumphal business tour of Wales in 1802, visiting the Cyfarthfa Ironworks to thank them for their critical role in the war effort and checking the manufacture of HMS Victory's cannonballs, one of which was fired in celebration, killing a small boy.

Cardiff Bay is unrecognisable now from the time a vast tonnage of iron and coal came down the Taff Valley to the docks. John Crichton Stuart, the first Marquis of Bute built the first dock, in 1839, then the largest masonry dock in the world. At this time Merthyr Tydfil was over three and a half times the size of Cardiff.

Goods moved downstream from Merthyr first on the Glamorganshire Canal (1794), promoted by Richard Crawshay, complemented by the Pendarren Tramway, on which Trevithick ran the first ever steam locomotives in 1804, nicknamed 'Puffers' or 'Dragons'. Brunel was subsequently employed to build the Taff Valley Railway. The second Marquis added four more docks and became known as the 'creator of modern Cardiff', for no other commercial city in Britain was built on the land of just one family.

Merthyr, further up the Taff Trail, was described in the 1863 Bradshaw Guide; 'By

Industrial and dockland heritage reminders at Cardiff Bay

day the town is dirty, without order or management, with no supply of water and the only buildings of note are the Barracks and the vast Poor-house. By night it is spectacular [with 50+ blast furnaces]. Cholera and fever are rampant.' Bradshaw remarks 'We hope that proper measures will be taken henceforth by those who draw enormous wealth from working these works, to improve the condition of the people.'

So, of course, the Taff Trail deserves iconic status. Remembering why is a little more tricky.

Other local cycle trails

The Green Lady Trail takes you from the Taff Trail at Nantgarw, traffic free through woodland into Caerphilly and on to the Bedwas to Machen cycle path.

The Two Parks Trail is a 10 mile traffic free ride from the Taff Trail at Quakers Yard to the Parc Penallta and on up to Hengoed. From where there's a traffic-free path to Newport.

The Taff Trail itself continues through Pontypridd and Merthyr Tydfil and on past the Pontsticill reservoir for another 25 miles along forest tracks and open moorland, sometimes on rough tracks and with steep sections, over to Talybont-on-Usk and to Brecon. You need to check that the Brecon Beacons Bike Bus still operates for the return journey. A pack of strip maps for the full 55 mile (89 k) route is available from Sustrans.

A few years ago Sustrans Cymru issued a Code of Conduct for the Taff Trail in Cardiff in the hope of reducing conflict between cyclists, pedestrians and dog walkers, a Code which, it was pointed out by some cyclists, should apply equally to all users of the Trail. Recently the Council launched Enfys, a cycling network for Cardiff, and it is hoped that a connected network will result. A map is available from *www.keepingcardiffmoving.co.uk*.

1. The Senedd – the parliament of Wales;
2. Blackweir; 3. Taff Trail near Castell Coch;
4. Castell Coch

5. Afon Lwyd Trail / Llwybr Afon Lwyd

Cwmbrân to Blaenavon (*Blaenafon*)

Distance: *29 km / 18 m*
OS Map: *1:50,000*
          171 Cardiff and Newport
          161 Abergavenny and The Black Mountains
Leaflet: *Sustrans Afon Lwyd Trail*
Access and Parking:
          Cwmbrân
          Pontymoel
          Pontypool
          Blaenavon
Surface: *Tarmac*
Nearby places of interest:
          Blaenavon World Heritage Site
          Big Pit: National Coal Museum
          Pontypool and Blaenafon Railway
          Pontypool Park and Museum

He was wearing a flat cap, shirt sleeves rolled up, braces, and riding an old bike with the comfort of a long marriage. 'I'm a fair weather cyclist', he said, and went on to tell us of all the rides he could take locally. He would ask, 'you know Llammarch?' and 'Twyn Ffynhonnau Oerion?' and take my blank look as an affirmative. We were over a thousand feet up, looking out over the moors and he waved 'ta-da' and rode off up the lane.

The Afon Lwyd Trail is not really one trail but parts of two separate trails, connected by some messing about in Pontypool as the cyclist has to negotiate a bad case of the ubiquitous South Wales disease, the carving through the Valleys of new, multi-lane highways, but both parts are refreshing and fun.

'Where am I?' 'Pontnewydd.' 'And where's Cwmbrân?' 'It's all Cwmbrân.' It feels like the countryside, fish in shoals, water boatmen, a paradise for ducks. This is '49', basically a canal towpath ride from Newport to Brecon, at Pontnewydd non-navigable due to broken locks and in parts a complete absence of water. From Cwmbrân Station it's uphill. Ignore the signs '492'. It is lovely and friendly with amblers and saunterers lost in reverie. The cafe at Pontymoel Basin is in an old boat and the proprietress good for a chat. She'll

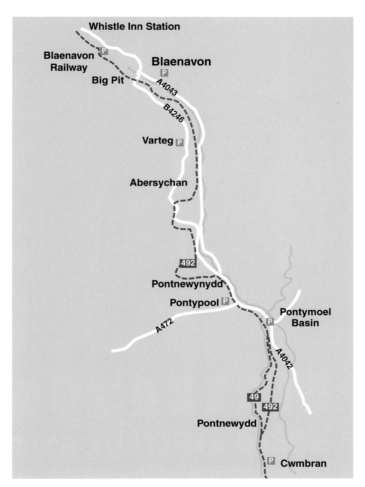

BLAENAVON
WORLD HERITAGE SITE

SAFLE TREFTADAETH BYD

put you right. Cyclists get confused, she says, as if talking about ancient doolally aunts. Backtrack a little and this time join '492', the old railway track from Cwmbrân all the way up to Blaenavon, except for Pontypool of course. Annie says, How come whenever a cyclepath runs alongside a road there's litter?

At Pontnewynydd you're free, a tarmac path all the way up to the Whistle Inn (recommended by flat cap and braces), high on the hillside floating along through oak woodland, chatting to locals and all the time quietly climbing, though you hardly notice. Apart from D.W.s in the villages there's just yourself and the birds for much of the time, and to think that not so long back coal and iron in enormous quantities came along here. For the last few miles the track has been retained, with Runnings at weekends (saddle tanks and a Co-Co 31 diesel named Steve Organ G.M.).

Back in the 1980s, after the DJ played Riders on the Storm for us on our wedding night, Annie and I honeymooned on Narrowboat Jade travelling first through Shipley, Barnoldswick and Wigan, with the industry fast disappearing, leaving unemployment and empty factories, and

we described the towns as a 'living museums'. The phrase is now used to describe places like Blaenavon, and if you ask what it means, the answer is a drawer full of questions, like:

-Is it comfortable and clean, or should it reflect reality?

-Is it for locals, or visitors? 'Us' or 'them'?

-Is it to educate or entertain?

-How can it not be political?

If you ask people in the know they talk of a shared heritage, interpretation, integration and a community gathering centre for experiences, tradition, for co-operation, collaboration and imagination. Americans talk of 'Art Museums' for Art Galleries; when does the past start? Surely a 'living museum' is as much about now as then? These questions hang in the air above Blaenavon much as the muck did in the old days.

Cwmbrân

Planners love New Towns. They like the idea of being able to shape communities, of patterns and order and control. In 1946 Cwmbrân was nominated as Wales' New Town, a Mark One New Town, part of the new planning system, and planners' eyes glazed over at the prospect of many generations to come. Cwmbrân is decreed a major success, with it's zoning, 'balanced' community, pedestrian-friendly car-and-bus-based design. None of the New Towns were designed for the bicycle. I'm putting up my hand for I was a planner, for five years before the anarchist in me gained the upper hand.

Cwmbrân existed before 1949. The Blewitts developed brick making, lime kilns, coal and iron ore mining and quarrying, making full use of the canal and two railways. In 1900 the Patent Nut and Bolt Co. became part of GKN. Now Cwmbrân makes Jammie Dodgers, Wagon Wheels and aircraft seats. A railway station arrived in 1986. The New Towns were supposed to be radical and utopian. Planners, by and large, are middle-class and conservative.

Pontypool (*Pont-y-pŵl*)

Richard Hanbury was a banker, described as 'aggressive'. He even served time for fraud. In the C16th he built a blast furnace in Pontypool and the industry grew, peaking during the Napoleonic Wars, specialising in japanning. It was Major John Hanbury who sent his agent 'disguised as a buffoon' to learn the secret of polishing iron and applying lacquer, rendering it rustproof and capable of carrying water, and who then developed a range of domestic tinware.

Major John moved into Pontypool Park House, built by his father, and surrounded it with 158 acres of parkland, to be transformed into a public park in 1920, including the Grotto, built for family picnics and during shoots, and decorated with shells by Molly.

Going north, Abersychan, Varteg and Forgeside were all industrial communities, iron and coal.

The old ironworks at Blaenavon

Blaenavon (*Blaenafon*)
(World Heritage Site)

Big Pit, the remains of the ironworks, the network of tramroads, watercourses and reservoirs, the spectacular quarries and that massive area of twisted, torn, prodded and probed landscape dominating the skyline above the town are enduring memorials to the role of the great unsung of history. The countless numbers of people who lived around the mines, quarries and ironworks were some of the true makers and creators of Britain as the first industrialised nation in the world.'

Richard Keen, Introduction to the book *Exploring Blaenavon* by Chris Barber (Blorenge, 2002).

In 1796 the Blaenavon Ironworks was the largest producer of iron in Wales, exported along the Trail upon which you have just ridden. In 1980 the Ironworks and Stack Square were saved from the bulldozer only because the Town Council hoped they could be used as a film set, and when the Big Pit finally closed in the 1990s the question was asked, "Can we build a future on the past?"

Other local cycle routes

www.torfaen.gov.uk has excellent route maps for both North and South Torfaen, including some feeder routes into the Big Three trails. Afon Lwyd is one. The second is NCN 49, Newport to Abergavenny, along the towpath of the Monmouthshire and Brecon Canal, isolated from the rest of the canal network but one of the most beautiful. Further down towards Newport the Fourteen Locks Canal Centre is part of the project to restore to navigation this part of the canal. Lastly NCN 466, Pontypool to Ebbw Vale, is a work in progress. From Pontypool to Crumlin is open, a mixture of off and on road; Ebbw Vale to Cwm is off road and open, but the section in the middle has yet to be completed.

Heads of the Valleys. Another work in progress. Consult *www.sustrans.org.uk/ncn/map* for the on and off road sections in this part of the world. I think that one day this will be a cycling Mecca, once the Powers-that-be stop fantasising about the glorious sweeping Heads of the Valleys motorway, and the £375 million Circuit of Wales proposed for Ebbw Vale.

Alternatively you could bump into Mr Flat Cap and Braces and ask, he'd be only too willing to share his knowledge.

'Big Pit'
the National Coal Museum at Blaenavon

6. Clydach Gorge

Abergavenny (Llanfoist) to Brynmawr

Distance: 13 km / 8 m
OS Map: 1:50,000
161 Abergavenny and The Black Mountains
Leaflet: Trail information available at the Sustrans website
Access and Parking:
Llanfoist Crossing
Gilwern
Brynmawr
Surface: Mostly tarmac with one rough hardcore section
Nearby places of interest:
Blaenavon Industrial Landscape
Big Pit: National Coal Museum
Abergavenny Castle and Museum
Pontypool and Blaenavon Railway

Another railway path, this time part of the Merthyr, Tredegar and Abergavenny Railway, AKA Heads of the Valleys Line. The previous two runs have been down the valleys to the sea. This was the breakout railway line, the alternative route to and from the South Wales coalfield and ironworks. It is spectacular. The Clydach Gorge is in the Brecon Beacons National Park, it has also been included in the Forgotten Landscapes Project.

Unfortunately this trail is in metamorphosis.

Like the transformation of a baby hedgehog from a wrinkly, stubbly, pink ball into the iconic creature we know and love, so will the Clydach Gorge trail transform from the deformed route we have now into a thing of beauty and majesty. It is halfway there already.

Begin at the Llanfoist Crossing Car Park. Such simple words. The 'Car Park' is on the right a half mile up the road to Blaenafon. Believe in the 'P' indicators. The trail signage is '46', nothing else. As you join it the old railway track is already climbing, and does so for the next eight miles, as steeply as 1 in 34. It is a beautiful steady climb through woodland, crossing after a while, the Brecon and Abergavenny Canal (see Trail 5 Afon Lwyd) and passing through Govilon Station. The views to the

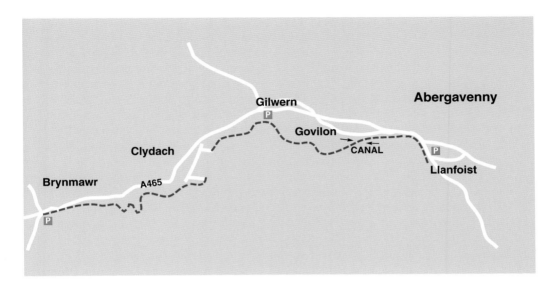

Beacons and Sugar Loaf and Skirrid Mountains gradually open out before the line turns into the dramatic Clydach Gorge. Quarries appear, and tunnels as the line works its way into the steepening gorge. At one point the trail is on a winding path across a rock face with sheer cliffs above and below.

At the time of writing the trail is struggling, firstly from a diversion onto steep narrow lanes to skirt a section of line to which access has been denied by a "bloody minded" owner, to quote a neighbour. A campaign is in full swing to rectify this. The second deformity comes courtesy of the Welsh Office as the A465 below is converted into a high grade dual carriageway. Not only is the peace of the valley rent by huge mountain moving machinery, but the end of the trail towards Brynmawr is being redesigned in the process, with another diversion in place in the meanwhile. It is hoped that, by the time you ride this trail, it will indeed be iconic.

The cycle path follows partly the old railway line and partly the previous tramroad. You'll pass old workings: two pairs of lime kilns from the Llanelly Limeworks; another two pairs from the Clydach Limeworks, built to provide lime for the construction of the nearby Nant Dyar Viaduct; lime kilns from the Blackrock Limeworks, worked until 1908; and the remains of the furnace from the Clydach Ironworks. In 1841 over 1350 people were employed here. The rough section has been left so deliberately as the railway track bed contains rare grassland fungi.

The path ends in Brynmawr, where you will encounter the Crawshay Bailey Trail, a 5½ mile hike.

Joseph Bailey, nephew of Richard Crawshay ('The Iron King') bought Nantyglo Ironworks from the Blaenavon Iron Co. with his brother, and set about buying other ironworks and sinking coal mines in and around Blaenavon. Joseph retired early to become landed gentry, leaving the business to his younger bro., Crawshay Bailey ('The Last of the Great Iron Kings'). He invested in coal and railways; he loved grime and smoke, steam and soot (don't we all? sigh) and would not be tempted by manors or parks or castles. He left everything to his illegitimate son, Crawshay Bailey Junior ('The Squire of Maindiff'), who married a Greek Countess and devoted himself to foxhunting.

Crawshay Bailey retired to Llanfoist House and there he died. His grave in St. Faith's Church in Llanfoist is crowned with an obelisk, and inside the church he has a stained glass window, placed there by Crawshay Bailey Jnr., AKA Crawshay Baker Bailey, which has the ring of a seventies country rock band.

When Joseph and Crawshay Bailey took joint ownership of the Nantyglo and Beaufort Ironworks they used tramroads to ship raw materials in and iron out. Three of these ran to wharves on the Brecknock and Abergavenny Canal, at Gilwern, Govilon and Llangattock. The oldest (1793) was the Clydach Railroad, which Crawshay converted to standard gauge in 1860. The engineer was John Gardner (London and Greenwich Railway;

Stack Square heritage cottages at Blaenavon

Newport Docks) and the line was one of the most heavily engineered in Wales (and therefore most expensive), with a nine mile climb as steep as 1 in 34, tunnels, tight curves and a hillside shelf.

Financial problems during construction in 1861 saw the LNWR (London and North Western Railway) take a 1,000 year lease on the railway line. Other railway companies, GWR, TVR and several other independents dominated South Wales at the time and the LNWR wanted a slice of the action. This was it. At its peak in the 1930s they ran twelve passenger services each day on this line, with through coaches from Cardiff via Rhymney Bridge to Crewe, Liverpool and Manchester. A GPO mail sorting van ran from Euston via Shrewsbury to Merthyr. LNWR used workaday engines, Webb Coal

Tanks (0-6-0) and latterly LMS Ivatt Class 2S (2-6-2T), but the line was difficult to use efficiently. In 1958 passenger services were withdrawn and goods trains stopped in 1971.

Abergavenny.

The castle is Norman, built for William the Conqueror by Hammeline de Balun to guard this pass into Wales. Should Wales gain independence when England leaves the EU there will be a customs post here.

The town specialised in Welsh wigs, made from goats hair, and very expensive. When will wigs make a comeback?

The other castle, Clytha, is a memorial to Elizabeth Jones, built in the Gothic style by her husband to mourn her passing in 1787. Good idea, we could all do this, it would solve the housing shortage.

Other local cycle trails

Perhaps because of its proximity to The Tumble, Abergavenny has a Festival of Cycling, with a Criterium and other races, and also a fun ride.

In addition to the aforementioned Afon Lwyd and Mon. and Brec. Canal routes, and the wonderful potential for cycling along the Heads of the Valleys to Merthyr and beyond, Abergavenny lies at the junction of two Sustrans routes, 42 and 46. 42 is on quiet roads from Hay-on-Wye down to Chepstow, with, to be honest, quite a few challenging climbs. This route was included in my Lands End to John O'Groats cycle guide, but I was only expecting it to be used by those End to Enders with more time than most, and strong legs. The Sustrans route is not yet a finished run. Neither is Route 46 along the Heads of the Valleys to Hereford.

7. The Peregrine Path / Llwybr yr Hebog

Monmouth (*Trefynwy*) to Symonds Yat / Saracens Head

Distance: 8 km / 5 m
OS Map: 1:50,000
162 Gloucester and Forest of Dean
Leaflet: Sustrans The Peregrine Path (423)
Access and Parking:
Monmouth and Symonds Yat The Biblins
Surface: Hardcore
Nearby places of interest:
Monmouth
The Kymin and Naval Temple
Castles at Chepstow, Goodrich, Grosmont, Raglan, Skenfrith and the White Castle near Llantillo.
Notes: Saracens Head ferry runs all year round, except in times of flood. Adults 80p, child 40p, cycle 40p.
Path managed by the Forestry Commission and Sustrans.

A lovely, short, gliding path through woodland, darkening towards Saracens Head as the valley narrows. It is a rare treat to be able to cycle care-free and traffic-free on the banks of a river, but take note, if your offspring is reckless or prone to mindlessness, the path is unfenced and at times of flood the Wye is mighty. I include this warning at Annie's insistence (having initially pooh-pooh'd the idea on the grounds that we all should learn the hard way). She also asks me to point out that the path crosses the English border ("It may be important"), where exactly is not clear though Annie claims to be able to spot the difference, but then she has also been chased down a Pembrokeshire lane by a UFO.

Note that the path is dual use and pedestrians abound, often insouciantly transported to a higher plane with their heads in the clouds, and warnings of your approach need to be clear and concise, though where exactly "Gwyliwch allan, agosáu ar gyflymder" should be spoken in English is not exactly clear, though Annie would know of course.

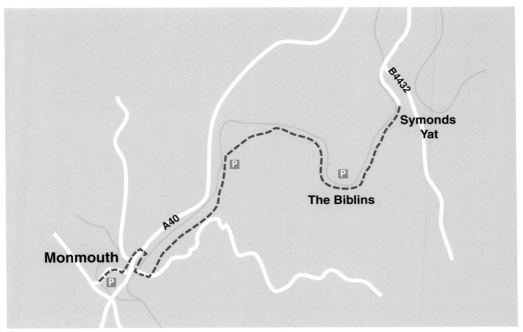

Given the choice I would start at the Monmouth end. Monmouth itself is yet another town which rolls over when the motor vehicle whistles, which is a real shame for it has a good deal going for it, and in another life it could be a real gem. Not least because it has one of the Fun Museums of Britain. Based on the enthusiastic collecting of memorabilia of Admiral Horatio Nelson, following his stay chez Lady Llangattock in the company of Sir William and Lady Hamilton (though where Emma slept is not clear, Sir William was twice her age, and Nelson had already lost an arm and most of his teeth). The exhibits include Nelson's swords, sailcloth from the Victory, seats known to have been in contact with the Nelsonian posterior, his glass eye (perhaps found in the morning after their departure in a glass of water by his bedside?), locks of the Admiral's hair tied with pretty ribbons, and a lock taken from his head as he lay on the deck of the Victory dying and matted, still, with Horatian blood. I should perhaps mention that other museums are available, of a more sober nature. Nelson came to Monmouth in 1802 on his triumphal business trip, essentially to meet with the timber merchants of the Wye Valley to ensure supplies of oak for the shipyards of Portsmouth and Plymouth.

For the inexperienced cyclist avoid Monmouth, but you can start from Hadnock Road, and there are three miles or so of quiet road passing a forgotten factory or two, then alongside the River Wye (all the while trying to ignore the rumble of the A40 on the opposite bank). This inauspicious start is soon shaken off, indeed you can drive it if you must and seek one of the two small car parks placed handily for the walkers of dogs. Take note: this is one of the least well signed of these cycle trails, though the way is straightforward: look for the small Sustrans signs No. 423. (At the Saracen's Head end the path is marked Forestry Commission, High Meadow Woods.) The next three miles are glorious. Note the scuffling on the verges, to which we will return. The path itself is hardcore, flat and easy.

Hadnock Halt was a request stop on the Ross to Monmouth Railway provided by the GWR for locals in 1951. The sidings served local iron ore and coal mines. The original Biblins Suspension Bridge was built in 1957, and from here on in pedestrian traffic increases. Saracens Head provides what Annie calls a "destination", ice cream and a pub. There are also canoes, cavers, river boat trips, a hand-hauled ferry, campsite, and high on the cliff a nest of peregrine falcons. There used to be more! The Danter fairground now at Stourport on Severn was here until 2010.

The Royal Forest of Dean
The river Wye is one boundary of the Forest of Dean. The valley itself is a designated SSSI, with unpolluted water

Grosmont castle, built by the Norman lords

The Peregrine Path by the Wye river

famed for salmon. If you're lucky you'll also see kingfishers, pied flycatchers, redstarts, wood warblers, hawfinches and all manner of butterflies and dragonflies, hawks too, goshawks and falcons. The Forest is a designated National Forest Park, with vestiges of the traditional industries, iron working (by one of the Crawshay clan), coal mining and charcoal burning.

It became a royal hunting forest in Norman times when this border country was given to powerful French lords who built castles and were given free rein to subdue the Welsh. For centuries the Forest was a source of venison and boar for royal dining tables. The number of fallow deer in the forest has varied considerably, with a maximum of around 800 deer, affected by poaching and changes to cover, especially after the Enclosures. By 1855 they were all gone, mainly to poachers as rural poverty became widespread. After the 39-45 War they were reintroduced, and with the absence of people during the year of foot and mouth disease, they spread throughout the Forest. About 60 are killed each year in road accidents, winter culling keeps their numbers down, with some controversy about 'trophy hunting', but in

2015 the BBC reported that poaching was again 'out of control', and the ITV called it an 'epidemic'.

So we return to the scuffling, which you've guessed by now, are the marks of the other contentious resident, the wild boar. They became extinct in England at least 300 years ago, but escapees and deliberate releases from wild boar farms have led to a feral, breeding population in the Forest of Dean. They can be large and unpredictable. When defending their young females will snort and make a fuss and may make a mock charge (so how do you know when a charge is mock?). Males are often indifferent to people but they have been known to attack dogs. Most injuries to humans from wild boar occur when the boar have been hit by a car. Some locals dislike them for the nuisance they cause in rooting about in playing fields and on golf courses, and they cause disturbance at night, not specifically the wild boar, but the local dogs barking at them. Initially it was recommended that numbers be stabilised at around 90, by trained marksmen, traffic fatalities and private landowners shooting them for the table, but they like it here. Numbers are estimated at over 1600 and growing by more than 300 a year. Culling is contentious, but we are their only predator, and how many thousand other farm animals are killed in the Forest each year? On the other hand it is good to see 'nature' fighting back, and what are we doing anyway farming 'wild' boar?

Snippets

Symonds Yat. A yat is Old English for a gate, and still part of every Cumbrian's vocabulary. Robert Symonds of Sugwas and Evesfield was a local landowner and Gentleman and High Sheriff of Herefordshire in 1685.

The Saracens Head. A common symbol in heraldry, possibly indicating the participation of an ancestor in the Crusades, although it is also thought possible that there may have been implicit support for Oliver Cromwell in the Civil War, owing to Charles' swarthy complexion.

8. Elan Valley Trail / Llwybr Cwm Elan

Rhayader (*Rhaeadr Gwy*)

Distance: *14.5 km / 9 m*
OS Map: *1:50,000*
          147 Elan Valley and Builth Wells
Access and Parking:
          Rhayader
          Elan Valley Visitor Centre
          Pont ar Elan at the top of
          Penygarreg Reservoir
Surface: *Tarmac, then hardcore, roughish*
          in places and prone to muddy
          patches in downpours.
Nearby places of interest:
          Elan Valley Visitor Centre
          Carngafallt RSPB Reserve

At times on this valley trail there are reminders of the pre-reservoir era, and the life here during construction, but the stretch required to be made in your imagination is not an easy one, and few people live in the valley these days. The scale is dramatic. The Trail begins in Cwmdeuddwr near Rhayader with a slightly overgrown incline by which you gain access to the old Birmingham Corporation railway track bed. A pleasant, wooded path takes you to the Visitor Centre (café, cycle hire etc.) then up to the three original dams and reservoirs with a wonderful sense of wide, open spaces. The atmosphere is still and peaceful with just birdsong to listen to (red kite, wheatear, peregrine falcon, ring ouzel, pied flycatcher), broken only when your cycling companion submits to the temptation to hear her own voice echoing back across the valleys. The very quiet mountain road also climbs the valley, and it is hard to resist the temptation to float back down on the road on your return, past the middle reservoir.

The Shelley Link

Percy Bysshe Shelley was born in Sussex in 1792. (Questions You're All Asking #1: Bysshe? According to the Origin of Names book it derives from an English surname 'originally indicating a person who lived near a bush'. Really?? In Percy's case, his Granddad was called Bysshe). Shelley was the Justin Bieber of his day, with two

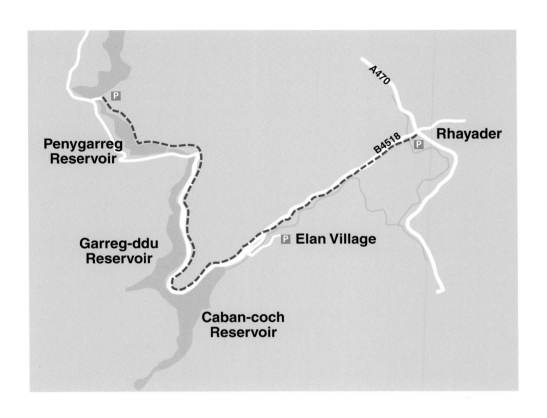

Penygarreg
Reservoir

Garreg-ddu
Reservoir

Caban-coch
Reservoir

Elan Village

Rhayader

A470

B4518

differences. Firstly he had talent, and secondly he packed more into his 29 years than Bieber ever will. His idyllic childhood abruptly ended at Eton, where he was 'tormented daily' by older pupils. I believe it is called nowadays, bullying. (QYAA #2: bullying? The origin is fascinating, but a diversion too far- see *promoteprevent.org*.) Shelley responded by electrifying his doorknob. At Oxford his promulgation of atheism, pacifism and vegetarianism got him thrown out and he was invited by his uncle to come and stay at Cwm Elan, now under the water you see before you. Shelley walked, from London (Bieber, are you reading this?) at the age of 18 and fell in love with the wild romantic landscape, and also with his cousin Harriet. But Harriet spurned his advances. Oh, he was heartbroken, and saved only when a letter arrived from an acquaintance, sixteen year old Harriet Westbrook. He shot back to London, they eloped immediately and married in Edinburgh, then moved into Nantgwyllt, just down the road from Cwm Elan, and now also under water. Nantgwyllt was a humble seven bedroomed abode, but haunted and also cheap. A dream home for the newlyweds.

But, In Every Dream Home a Heartache, it was not yet theirs, and his family refused to give Shelley his coming-of-age money. They had to leave. The pair moved to Porthmadog where Percy Bysshe was subject to an apparent attack, possibly because he criticised the locals for rearing sheep to eat, possibly because he failed to pay his debts. It has been suggested that his mysterious death off the coast of Italy was a retaliatory murder by disgruntled Welsh, but for that, tales of the other wives, girlfriends and 'utopian' friendships in the next ten years, and Shelley's input to Frankenstein, you will have to seek answers elsewhere.

Both Cwm Elan and Nantgwyllt are under water, except in years of exceptional drought.

Birmingham, bombs and Baroque

A little to the East, seventy three miles to be exact, Victorian Birmingham was growing apace. The City doubled in size in the fifteen years from 1876. Birmingham took its water from wells, which were becoming contaminated with sewage, just

Rhayader (Rhaeadr Gwy)

Iconic Cycling Trails in Wales

like some Third World cities today, and epidemics of water-borne diseases like typhoid, cholera and diarrhoea were not unusual. The City Fathers cast about for clean water and their eyes alighted upon the Elan and Claerwen valleys, with their plentiful rainfall, narrow (romantic) valleys, impermeable bedrock and higher elevation than Birmingham, enabling water to be supplied by gravity alone. (QYAA #3: Surely the valleys were already occupied? They were, by a hundred or so locals who were evicted without compensation or even a Government Rescue Package. The workhouse beckoned. The landowners were, of course, paid off.)

Work began in the 1890s with the construction of a railway, upon which the eight saddletank locomotives moved about a thousand tons of building materials each day, plus the workforce. The workers lived in the new Elan Village, made out of wooden huts, single men being housed in groups of eight to a house with a man and his wife, the inference being obvious though unpalatable to the modern woman (I'm talking food here).

Children joined the workforce at age eleven. During the thirteen years of construction over fifty thousand men were employed on site, many of them itinerant navvies. The village grew to over one and a half thousand people by 1898, with a hospital for injuries and one for isolation, a library, hall, shop, canteen and bathhouse, which men were allowed to use up to thrice a week, and women once. As well as the railway there were massive steam cranes, stone-cutting saws and crushing plants, all of which required water. So the first job was the high Nant-y-Gro dam to provide water for the village and storage tanks for the steam engines. When the Second World War came around this dam was still intact, and used by Barnes Wallis to test early versions of the bombs used by the Dambusters, including the bouncing bomb. (QYAA #4: Why didn't the Germans try to bomb these dams and deprive Birmingham of its water? Answer; I don't know.)

The dams, reservoirs and seventy three mile long aqueduct were opened in 1904 by King Edward the Seventh and Queen Alexandra (QYAA#5: Football in Crewe? Answer; the very same person). The huge

1. Elan Valley dam; 2. Craig Goch reservoir

Claerwen Dam was added in 1952 and recent proposals for a really, really big dam have been put on hold. The waterworks were built in the style of 'Birmingham Baroque', one of the Victorian revivalist styles. Baroque is characterised by the bizarre and irregular, almost theatrical.

Elan Village is no longer wooden huts, but was rebuilt by Herbert Buckland in the 'Arts and Crafts' style to house workers responsible for maintaining the dams and filtration systems. (QYAA #6: Architectural styles, boring, surely? Answer; We have been brutalised by concrete and side-tracked by functionalism. The job, looking ahead, is for every neighbourhood to be a pleasure to inhabit, so instead of coming to the Elan Valley to cycle, you can do so in safety and delight in your own locale).

Other local cycle trails

As far as I can tell there are no other comparable cycle trails locally. A few longer distance touring routes cross the region, but these are on local roads in the main. When I first went to Ireland back in the 1970s travel by any means was slow. On the roads donkey traps with milk churns heading for the nearest creamery often dictated speed, and the road menders simply dug up the road with shovel and pick and not a word of warning. It wasn't THAT different here. Something has happened in the meanwhile and the concept of shared road space has been negated by speeding and bullying traffic. Perhaps it should be a condition of the driving test that the learner should spend an hour cycling on the same roads.

Penygarreg reservoir

9. Montgomery Canal Greenway / Lôn Las Camlas Maldwyn

Welshpool (*Y Trallwng*) to Newtown (*Y Drenewydd*)

Distance: 23 km / 14½ m

OS Map: 1:50,000
126 Shrewsbury and Oswestry
136 Newtown and Llanidloes
137 Church Stretton and Ludlow

Leaflet: Sustrans 81 Montgomery Canal

Access and Parking:
Welshpool
Berriew
Abermule
Newtown

Surface: Smooth hardcore in the main, tarmac towards Newtown.

Nearby places of interest:
Montgomery
Welshpool and Llanfair Light Railway
Castell Powis
Castell Dolforwyn
Newtown

The Greenway runs along the canal towpath, though care is needed at the three road crossings of the busy A483, where canal bridges have been removed and the canal culverted. The route is like a stream of consciousness without the words, a linear wetland, half of it navigable though with hardly a boat, with constantly changing textures, stretches of lush tunnels of dappled trees, and at other times colourful cow-grazed water meadows. There is life aplenty, kingfisher, red kite, nesting swans, ducklings, shoals of fish and all manner of dragonfly. Sometimes the path is like walking a tightrope between the old (rusting tractors, corrugated iron canal buildings, rustic gardens, black and white houses, smallholdings, glimpses of lives lived) and the new (the occasional intrusion of modern farming) and all the while folks noisily chasing each other along the A483, which sometimes fades into the

1. & 2. Montgomery Canal and path

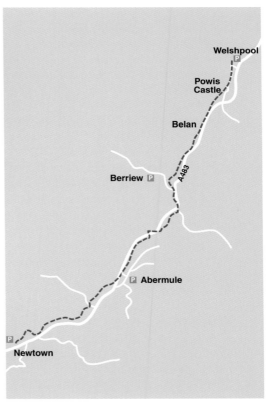

background, but at others requires you to suppress that particular sense.

Progress is of necessity slow, even more so towards the Newtown end, for soon after a tunnel the canal becomes a ditch, then turns into sheep pasture. From the sewage works into town the surface is tarmac and the route labelled 'Riverside Cycleway' and '81'. Most of the towpath is smooth hardcore (Annie says "Thank you"). She also describes the numerous bridge-holes as a "feature", and it is fun watching her eagerly keen not to miss a thing whilst ducking her head and trying to stay upright with the drink beckoning.

The last time we rode the Greenway we met hardly a soul, but just missed Derek the Walking Weatherman in the Powisland Museum.

Remembering;

Although it is thirty five years ago now since we lived on the cut, we've never really left, and we always intended going back. Back then a year of that time was spent at Buttington Wharf near Welshpool researching the Montgomery Canal and beginning a rudimentary museum. Narrowboat Jade was not always moored at Buttington of course, we had seven miles of navigable canal to play with, a seven mile long back garden. Some memories are crystal clear; the kingfisher on Jade's bow; the thick grass snake swimming alongside the skiff; eating breakfast watching a stoat hunt along the bank; the shoals of fish beneath the boat; sitting on the boat with month old Molly surrounded by the reflections of the wind rippling the water; tethering her to a mooring ring when she learned to crawl and watching her try to play with a hedgehog. It wasn't all a picnic. In the winter of '81 the valley was a lake of water as the Severn burst its banks, and in the winter of '82 N.B. Jade was half submerged in a snowdrift. We carried all our water from a tap and had no room inside to dry the washing, and every week I'd tie the elsan onto the bike trailer and pedal into town to empty it. I remember getting up with Annie in the night when Molly was hungry to light a candle and put some wood on the stove, or sods of peat we'd brought over from Whixall Moss. Living on the cut slows you down and toughens

1. Castell Powis; 2. Castell Dolforwyn

you up. The living space was twenty feet by six so much of our lives was outside. It was also very social, chatting to anyone passing, and there's the bush telegraph keeping you in touch with events up and down the cut. We learned from the clumps of cut weed that came floating by that a farmer up Berriew way had a blocked bath, for his bath water came direct from the cut and he'd told Roy, the Inspector, that it was time for the weedcutter.

NB Jade was luxurious compared to the old working boats on the Montgomery. The narrowboats were seventy two feet long and pulled by horses, donkeys or mules, with the boatman and his family living in a cabin ten feet by six feet ten inches, though towards the end of the canals' working life many boatmen kept a cottage 'on the bank'. Life could be hazardous, with pneumonia and other diseases, problems caused by the damp, stuffy cabins. Canal water was used for washing and the canal or hedgerow was the toilet. The boats were unloaded by hand. There was a knack in lifting a two hundredweight sack of grain from the boat to the wharf at Maesbury. Children were employed either steering the boat or walking behind the horse to prevent him

from grazing on the towpath. They also had to be nimble to avoid the inspectors trying to force them into school. Many of the babies were born in the boats themselves and often the woman would be back on the tiller two days later.

In August 1835 Pickfords began a flyboat service from London to Newtown. 'Flyboat' meant that the service was relatively speedy, which could only be achieved by travelling twenty four hours a day. Each boat had a crew of four men. There were regular changes of horses and the only illumination at night was a paraffin lamp. The Pickfords boats were granted special permission to travel at night for normally the locks would be padlocked to give the lock-keepers some sleep. In May 1837 the local lock-keepers accepted an extra two shillings and six pence to work nights.

The Welsh Canal

From Welshpool the canal passes the Powis Estate timber yard. The First Earl of Powis was Edward Clive, son of Clive of India. This wealthy estate benefited enormously from the canal, owning limestone quarries, lime kilns (the lime was used to fertilise the land) and flannel mills.

The long wharf at Berriew was owned by Charles Hanbury-Tracy, the First Baron Sudeley, a reforming MP and ironworks owner. He rebuilt Gregynog Hall in 1840 with concrete cladding to replicate the local timber framed farmhouses. Beyond that is the Vaynor wharf and limekiln. Vaynor Park still belongs to the Winder family.

Efail-Fach wharf (bridge 129) served the Glansevern Estate. Sir Arthur Davies Owen built the Hall in the Greek Revival style in 1801-6. It sold for £4.5m in 2013 and is famous for having the largest bathtub in Wales.

Garthmyl was the terminus of the canal during the Napoleonic wars. A total of seven wharves were built here, with thirteen lime kilns in three banks. In 1832 the kilns burned 6,956 tons of limestone with 2,250 tons of coal, all hauled here by boat.

The wharves at Pennant Dingle (bridge 143) belonged to William Pugh, who was born nearby in 1783. He became a radical landlord and entrepreneur, funding the extension of the canal to Newtown. He opened the first bank there, macadamised roads, introduced gas to the town, built the Flannel Market, began the newspaper and was the local rep. for the Society for the Diffusion of Useful Knowledge.

Aberbechan wharf (bridge 151) belonged to David Pugh of Llanerchydol Hall, tea trader, MP and military man.

The Montgomery Canal worked well for 140 years, through good times and bad, but then in the 1930s came the news. LTC Rolt in his famous book 'Narrow Boat' wrote,

> 'Next came news of a "burst". Part of the canal bank blew out on the western section of the Welsh Canal just below its junction with the arm that runs north to Llangollen over Telford's great aqueducts at Chirk and Pont-Cysyllte. It was not a serious matter, for canal lengthmen have since told me that it would have taken only a few days' work to restore the canal to navigable condition, but this was not to be.'

The breach, blamed on a burrowing mole or vole, occurred on 6 February 1936 when the canal, swollen with flood water, drained into the fields. The whole canal was abandoned in 1944. In the following years sixteen road bridges were flattened into the canal and the last two miles into Newtown filled in. A proposal to route a Welshpool by-pass along the line of the canal in 1969 was defeated by canal enthusiasts, who have worked ever since to restore the canal to navigation.

European grant aid and matching funding was pledged in 1988 for full restoration, but Conservative Secretary of State for Wales Peter Walker refused to give the go ahead, a devastating blow for the volunteers at that time.

The Montgomery Canal Greenway opened as a walking and cycling trail on 3 October 2013. Interestingly there is very little signage on the route but you can't really go wrong.

10. Llangollen Canal / Camlas Llangollen

Chirk to Horseshoe Falls

Distance: 15 km / 9 m

OS Map: 1:50,000
117 Chester and Wrexham
126 Shrewsbury and Oswestry
125 Bala and Lake Vyrnwy

Leaflet: Sustrans Llangollen Canal

Access and Parking:
Chirk
Froncysyllte (access only)
Trefor
Llangollen
Llantysilio Green

Surface: Trefor to Horseshoe Falls – hardcore
Trefor to Chirk – tarmac and hardcore

Nearby places of interest:
Llangollen
Chirk Castle
Ty Mawr Country Park
Valle Crucis Abbey
Eliseg's Pillar
Castell Dinas Bran

A slow mesmeric ride along the canal towpath between Chirk and Horseshoe Falls, passing even slower boats, with reflections in the water, cute ducklings and a picturesque landscape leading you stealthily into the jaws of the Dee Gorge.

Cycling along towpaths: Etiquette,

– Normally on these bike trails there is no set etiquette for passage, or 'rules of the road' as it were. Cyclists operate a creative anarchistic system, with some preferring a 'standard British' keep on the left rule, and others adopting a more Continental approach. I should say that Annie grew up in Massachusetts, if you should ever meet her on a trail, brace yourself. Towpaths can be scary things, you can meet all manner of obstruction, horses, fishermen, small boys, the leads of dogs, then there's the looming drink. Surprise dips can happen (especially when riding 'pillion' on the bike rack behind Barwise with one or two pints taken), but it is your duty as a respectable, honourable cycling towpath user to ride on the water side. A word of warning too. The sudden, close-up use of a 'charly' / 'ping' bell can cause alarm and

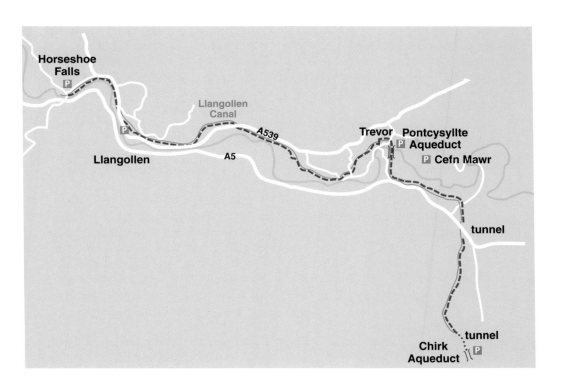

Horseshoe
Falls
P

Llangollen
Canal

A539

Trevor

Pontcysyllte
Aqueduct
P

P Cefn Mawr

Llangollen

A5

tunnel

tunnel
P

Chirk
Aqueduct

unpredictable panic, particularly among older, deafer Granddads, with potentially disastrous consequences. When approaching from behind prior warning is preferable, by whistling / idle banter / singing snatches of Hendrix.

Beginning at Chirk. After taking in the aqueduct and floating tuck-shop, the next move is a walk, through Chirk Tunnel. The water drips, it is dark, and if you should be lucky enough to catch a boat lighting the way, the tunnel soon resembles the Holloway Road at rush hour. We once, on board N.B. Jade forgot to let the fire go out before entering a tunnel, which was soon filled with fumes and smoke. There is a road over the top, but bear in mind that illogically the railway passes over the canal tunnel, and you'll need to cross the railway too to regain the towpath.

The cutting that follows can be a trifle muddy, but also delivers the heady combined aroma of pine and chocolate (no more Brut for me).

The Whitehouse Tunnel is shorter, and unavoidable. Thankfully there is a railing between you and the drink. Followed by a delightful meandering passage, then it's the 'Ponty'. We walked. It is not very wide.

Manoeuvrings are required at the Trefor basin as the towpath swaps side, then it is just a lovely towpath ride hung between the canal and the drop down to the valley below. I should also mention that it's a dog walkers paradise. As you ride along, if you want something to occupy your mind, remember that it was a favourite pastime of Llangollen ladies to stroll out and watch the navvies at work. Say no more.

Care and consideration are required towards Llangollen as footfall increases, particularly during the Eisteddfod in July. You may be lucky and catch a steam engine at work. The horse is called Hercules. Don't believe the waterways workers when they tell you that the fish swimming in the clear water are plaice and haddock.

The Ellesmere Canal (**Llangollen Canal**)
The idea for the Ellesmere Canal was conceived during 'Canal Mania', 1789-96, with the intention of linking the rivers Mersey, Dee and Severn, plus a branch through the broken country of the Welsh border via Ruabon with its coal mines and

Llangollen Canal and path

Iconic Cycling Trails in Wales

iron works. William Jessop was chief engineer, and he appointed the young Thomas Telford to oversee the work. The Ellesmere Canal was his first canal.

Thomas Telford ('Laughing Tam') was born in Eskdalemuir in 1757, not far from today's Buddhist monastery Kagyu Samye Ling. Raised on a sheep farm, Telford was a contemporary of Robert Burns. He left school at 14 to become an apprentice stonemason. Largely self-taught he moved to Edinburgh aged 23, met a pair of Scottish architects and secured work building Somerset House in London. There he met Sir William Pulteney, also from Dumfriesshire (a 'doonhamer'), and reputedly the richest man in Britain, who commissioned him to fashion a home from the Norman motte and bailey castle in Shrewsbury, and then found him work as Surveyor of Public Works in Shropshire. Telford never married, had no known living relatives, and lived for his work.

He made his name with the Pontcysyllte aqueduct and went on to build more canals (including the Caledonian), over a thousand bridges (including the Menai Suspension Bridge),

Pontcysyllte aqueduct

thousands of miles of roads (including the Holyhead Road) and many churches and harbours (including Katherines Dock in London). He is buried in Westminster Abbey.

The Ellesmere Canal posed two major engineering problems, the crossing of the rivers Dee near Ruabon, and the Ceiriog near Chirk. Telford and Jessop were keen to use iron and were friends with William "Merlin" Hazeldine, the owner of the Plas Kynaston Iron Foundry in nearby Cefn Mawr. For the Chirk Aqueduct (built 1801) they set the iron trough in masonry, but over the Dee they set the iron trough on hollow, tapering stone pillars, with a cantilevered towpath to allow water to flow past the moving boats. It is a World Heritage Site and the most impressive structure on the canal network, 1,007 feet long and 127 feet high. It took ten years to build, was completed in 1805 and cost £47,000. The iron trough was sealed with joints caulked with Welsh flannel (from Newtown) dipped in boiling sugar and ox blood, then sealed with lead.

The canal was abandoned in 1944, but maintained for its water supply to the rest of the network, though no maintenance

was done until 1963. Jack Strange (*Tales from the Old Inland Waterways* by Euan Corrie) was part of the maintenance team. They found no leaks in the trough and the thousands of nuts came off the bolts with just a tap of the hammer. He said, "It was a marvellous piece of work that aqueduct. They must have brought those plates by horse and cart from the foundry which was where Monsanto is now - but how did they get them across the top of those pillars...and how do you hold the next one there whilst you get the bolts through the flanges?"

The Llangollen branch was designed as a partially navigable feeder from the river Dee at Llantysilio (Horseshoe Falls). It was built with a clay channel, puddled, the channel itself built on compacted sand, and so breaches were a regular occurrence.

Until the arrival of the canal the local population was small. The Ellesmere Canal proper terminated at the Trevor Wharf, and soon there were four iron works locally, and local clay was used in the Plas Kynaston Pottery and several brick works. The impressive Cefn Mawr railway viaduct opened in 1848 for the Shrewsbury and Chester Railway Co. (later GWR) and in 1867 a chemical works was established at Plas Kynaston by the German Robert Graesser to extract paraffin oil and wax from local shale, an extension of Britain's 1860s 'oil-mania' centred between Falkirk and Edinburgh. The works expanded to include the production of coal tar and carbolic acid (phenol), with a wide range of uses including soap, shampoo, as a treatment for dandruff and head lice, paracetomol, pesticides and aspirin. Monsanto bought the company in 1919, and have left a site which is massively contaminated.

A horse-drawn trip boat began working the Llangollen Canal in 1884 and has continued ever since. The horse is stabled at Llangollen Wharf, where there is also an exhibition centre.
www.horsedrawnboats.co.uk

Snippets
Chirk (*Y Waun*)
Situated on the Welsh side of the border, the language is taught as a second

1. *Castell Dinas Brân above Llangollen;*
2. *Chirk castle;*
3. *Valle Crucis abbey*

language in the schools, though there are other Welsh-medium schools nearby.

The factories are Kronospan, a multinational company making roof trusses and MF and particle boards, and a factory for some of Mondelez International 'billion-dollar brands', Cadburys drinking chocolate, Dairy Milk, Crunchie and Creme Eggs.

1. & 2. Autumn colours along the canal;
3. Chirk aqueduct

11. North Wales Coastal Cycleway / Llwybr Arfordir Gogledd Cymru

Talacre to Llandudno
Sustrans National Cycle Network NCN5

Distance: *35 km / 22 m*
OS Map: *1:50,000*
116 Denbigh and Colwyn Bay
115 Caernarfon and Bangor
Cycle maps:
Sustrans 5 Conwy County Council (Llanfairfechan – Kinmel Bay)
Sustrans 5 Denbighshire (Rhyl – Prestatyn)

Access and Parking:
Throughout the length of the cycleway
Surface: *Mostly good, hard surfaces*

Notes: *The cycle path continues east to Mostyn. Sustrans NCN5 takes to the hills for a while on minor roads to avoid stretches of the A548. To the West NCN5 continues on the streets of Llandudno, then uses off road cycle paths to Llanfairfechan. It is a fun ride, with some climbing, around Great Orme's Head, free for cyclists.*

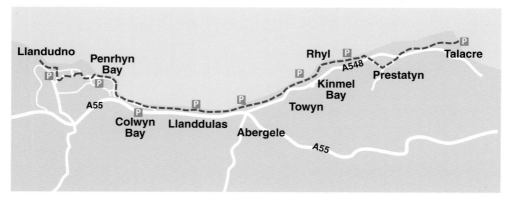

This is only one section of NCN5. It connects Reading at one end with Holyhead at the other. This section links all the towns along the North coast, the 'sunshine coast', with mostly traffic-free cycle paths, and is perfect for novices and families as well as more experienced cyclists. Parts are very popular. Much of the route is shared with pedestrians, particularly the promenades, so please show due consideration to those less fortunate than yourself. Annie says it is like being on a cruise ship, on a bike. There are opportunities for the sign-dyslexic to wander off into caravan favelas and bucket-and-spade construction sites, but generally it is a smooth flowing ride between land and sea, lulled by lapping waves and punctuated by bursts of raucous holiday-making. It is very popular with cyclists, did I already say that?

I should mention the one short steep hill near Llanddulas where the other jetty used to be, and the poor signage when approaching Prestatyn. Having successfully negotiated the golf course ('Cyclists Proceed with Caution; Danger from Flying Balls'), you need to take a right along Barkby Avenue to the sea, keeping to the seaward side of Pontins.

This is the whole holiday coast, from the DIY caravans and chalets of Talacre to the fashionable streets of Llandudno.

Along Llandudno's promenade

'The bicycle is one of the least known yet best and safest medicines that exist.'
Jean-Pierre de Mondenard MD 1977

Sea bathing is not new. There remains, in an obscure part of Prestatyn, the ruins of a Roman bath house, a small two-roomed bathhouse built around AD 120 for a wealthy family. Most centurions, I imagine, would just have charged down the beach into the sea, having left their armour in a neat pile above the tide line.

Before 1700 sea water was a well known treatment for gout but the whole business took off in 1750 when Dr Charles Russell published *A Dissertation concerning the Uses of Sea Water in Diseases of the Glands*. King George III (he of the 'madness') went to Weymouth, his son to Brighton. Sea bathing became fashionable. The word 'resort' is from the French, meaning a place of aid, and the medical profession being what it was, the practise was considered to be most effective by sea bathing in winter. In the 1930s Colwyn Bay was described as a 'Victorian resort increasingly in favour as a resort for individuals, during the coldest month of the year'. 'Prestatyn' is 'a rising resort with sunshine on about 324 of the 365 days of the year.' The most effusive praise was reserved for Rhyl, 'Rhyl's beaches are magnificent', with 'neither cliffs nor quicksands to place little visitors in danger.' The Open-Air Swimming Pool 'holds 775,000 gallons of water... There is cubicle accommodation for 400 bathers and provision for 5,000 spectators.' The Prince of Wales, later to become King George V, in 1902 spoke of the climate as "fine, healthy and bracing". Sir William Gull, MD, said, "I have on more than one occasion sent patients there, and especially for certain cardiac affectations." Dr Evans of Birmingham, a frequent visitor to Rhyl, said it was "unrivalled in the United Kingdom as a residence of consumptive patients." In more recent times the punk-poet, the 'Bard of Salford', John Cooper Clarke was sent to live with his Auntie Eileen in Rhyl to recover from childhood TB. Another poet, Kay Buckley, paints a different picture,

Rainy Rhyl. Welsh slate skies and sea the colour of cold bath water
(*From Rainy Rhyl*)

Towards Colwyn Bay

George the Fifth's mother, when Princess of Wales, laid the foundation-stone for the Royal Alexandra Hospital for Children, paid for by donations, including the prize money, £10,000, for the Eclipse Stakes at Sandown Park won for the Duke of Westminster by Flying Fox. The Flying Fox weathervane is still there on the "Alex".

Alexandra's husband, later King Edward the Seventh, was also a regular visitor to Rhyl, on his way to Ruthin to visit his lover, Mary Adelaide Virginia Thomasina Eupatoria Cornwallis-West, known to her husband as Mussie, and everyone else as Patsy. Ruthin Castle later became a private clinic specialising in obscure internal disorders including ulcers, gallstones and emaciation, and 'the maintenance of health in those who had no disease' (many of the patients suffered from 'hypochondriacal tendencies'). Treatment included croquet, fishing and 'mild' rounds of golf. Winter sea bathing was strictly for the working classes.

In 1848 mainland Europe was in revolutionary turmoil; famine in Ireland caused the death of a million people with another million forced to emigrate; and W H Smith opened their first railway shop. Off Abergele the Ocean Monarch caught fire and sank. She was carrying emigrants to America, 178 died. Rhyl railway station opened. Forty years previously it had been a marsh, which was drained and the plots sold, cheap housing rubbing shoulders with the elegant. In 1848 there were more than a thousand Rhyllians, by 1861, three thousand. Down the coast the Honourable E. M. L. Mostyn, MP, was putting the final touches to a plan for a 'first-class watering-place', which was to become Llandudno. All along this coast, to counter the dreadful conditions in the newly industrialised cities in Lancashire and the Midlands, landowners began to profit from new 'health resorts'.

Snippets
Talacre

Despite the presence of new holiday lodges, an atmosphere remains of the shanty town, for during the Second World War Liverpool families were evacuated here to live in old railway coaches and wooden huts, under the Spitfires using the beach as a firing range. Today the dunes are a nature reserve, home to the only breeding colony of little terns in Wales, and famous for its marsh and pyramidical orchids.

Talacre Hall was built in 1829, the home of the local gentry, the Mostyn baronets, until 1921 when a group of Benedictine nuns moved in.

A lighthouse here was the first to be built in Wales, though the present one dates from 1819. It has a reputation for the paranormal, with those who come too close affected by mysterious illnesses. A sculpture, 'The Keeper' was placed on the balcony in 2010, designed to moan in the wind.

A tidal barrage has been mooted from Talacre to Heswall, for power, with a road on top, potentially bringing this whole area into the commuter belt for Liverpool.

Presthaven Beach Resort, Gronant

A Haven resort, the acme modern holiday centre, with pools and loads of stuff for kids to do.

Prestatyn

There are plans to 'revitalise' the sea-front after a period of decline, including the Nova Centre. Pontins' Prestatyn Sands camp is one of the remaining five from around thirty original post-war holiday camps. The plan is for Disneyfication.

Rhyl

The Marine Lake was also the home of a fairground and zoo. The Ocean Beach Funfair dates from the 1890s and has had a huge variety of roller-coasters, dodgems, waltzers, ghost trains, kamikaze, breakdance, twist and rotor rides. It closed in 2007, leaving two other local fun fairs, Knightlys and Tir Prince at Towyn.

The Sun Centre cost £4.25m when it was built in 1980. Blown sand piles up at its doors as it awaits demolition following its demise in 2014.

The Sky Tower closed in 2010. Its future is uncertain.

A regeneration plan is in place, including a new aquatic centre and an exhibition centre. The cafe near Pont y Ddraig is something of a Mecca for cyclists.

Colwyn Bay

The new Eirias Watersports Centre is the face of future holidays. The past is the Victoria Pier, a decaying relic of a golden era. The Pavilion was opened in 1934 complete with Art Deco murals, and made fireproof (the old one burned down) with asbestos in the roof, walls and floor. Its future is also uncertain: restoration could

cost up to £15m; demolition £2.2m (the bequest of the modern world includes asbestos, toxic chemicals and nuclear waste, sorry kids); and part demolition, leaving the ironwork as an 'art installation' (surely art is created by an artist?).

Llandudno

The pier (1877m) is the longest in Wales, designed to be used at all states of the tide by paddle steamers from Liverpool. The last regular sailings were to the Isle of Man in the 1980s.

Castell Gwyrch, Abergele

Built 1812-22 by Lord Hesketh Bamford-Hesketh on the site of a ruined Elizabethan manor, some of it as a folly. The estranged husband of his granddaughter (keep up), the Twelfth Earl of Dundonald (big in the Boer War) purchased the house in 1928 for £78,000 and stripped the fittings to cover the cost. In the War it housed 200 Jewish refugees. In 1946 the Thirteenth Earl sold it for £12,000 and for 20 years it became 'The Showplace of Wales', attracting millions of visitors. Randolph Turpin and Bruce Woodcock trained here, there were jousting matches and motorcycle rallies. It closed in 1985 (a Californian bought it in 1989 to turn it into an opera house) and has since then been ravaged by the weather, vandals and New Age travellers. It is now on the way to restoration, www.gwrychtrust.co.uk.

Sea Defences

No-one knows by how much the sea will rise due to climate change. Estimates vary from half a metre to two metres by 2100. North Wales is planning for a one metre rise. This coast is very vulnerable and much has already been done, with concrete promenades and barriers in the towns, a long stretch of 'dolos', the twisted H-shaped cast concrete units (there are 22,000) and rock armour (riprap – the piles of stones) designed to absorb wave energy. A new practise is 'beach nourishment', the mechanical pumping of sand from offshore back onto the beaches. Will it be enough? We don't know.

The Great Orme Tramway and Llandudno bay

12. Lôn Las Ogwen

Porth Penrhyn (Bangor) to Llyn Ogwen

Distance: *18 km / 11 m*
OS Map: *1:50,000*
115 Caernarfon and Bangor
Leaflet: *Gwynedd Recreational Routes (Gwynedd Council)*
Access and Parking:
Porth Penrhyn
Tregarth
Bethesda
Idwal Cottage
Surface: *Tarmac and hardcore*
Nearby places of interest:
Bangor
Menai Bridge
Llanberis, two railways, the Electric Mountain and Slate Museum
Caernarfon

What a marvellous contraption is the bicycle. With a little effort, and some camaraderie, it can carry you from the barnacle-scraping and caulking of mariners preparing for adventures on the high seas, to rope-clad climbers attempting Suicide Wall and Invisible Thread on Idwal Slabs.

Lôn Las Ogwen has been pieced together from four contrasting route sections, but the lack of coherence is more than compensated by the drama. Think of it as a play in four acts with the stage hands having to work a little harder at each change of scenery.

Act One begins at Porth Penrhyn near the City of Bangor with its fine assortment of working and pleasure boats, perhaps eavesdropping outside the circular 12-seater Gents on the Quay, for the door is locked and your curiosity remains unslaked. The plot takes you past the gates of Castell Penrhyn along the gently inclined track of the tramway built to carry slate for export, through the sylvan valley of Afon Cegin, isolated from the surrounding estates. Through cuttings, over embankments and a mini-viaduct the trail emerges onto a village street in Tregarth. A further section of railway path, beginning opposite the lovely Capel Shiloh (the prophetic name for the Messiah, as in Shiloh Jolie-Pitt) ends at the mouth of the railway tunnel, alas now sealed off. End of Act One.

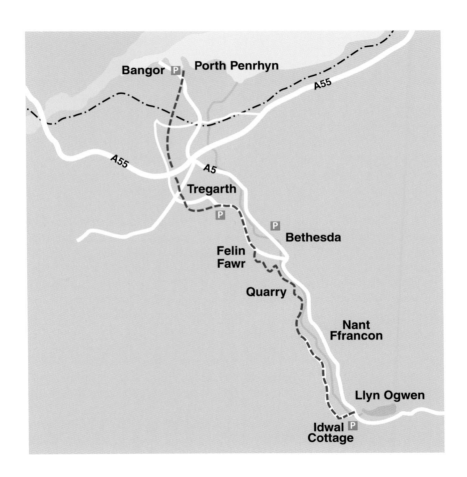

Act Two begins with a short sharp pull up back onto the B4409, the Hên-durnpike which you left at Capel Shiloh, and I mention this because at this point you don't know where you are, the mountains are ahead, the sea far behind and the village seemingly adrift. This was the old turnpike road to Bangor superseded by Telford's Holyhead Road on the other side of Afon Ogwen. It's a mile or so of roadwork, with the odd lane branching off steeply to the right to hillside quarry villages collectively known as Mynydd Llandegai. Act Two ends at Felin Fawr, the former slate works at the head of the Penrhyn Quarry Railway. The oldest building here dates from 1803. They were used as slab mills, loco sheds and a foundry. Restoration is in progress, with occasional Runnings.

Act Three takes place on hardcore tracks through the workings, with massive tailings rising abruptly from the track. Imagination is required from the glimpses you receive, but even so the scale of this quarry is difficult to comprehend. I should mention that the peace is disturbed at regular intervals by overhead screeching from the zip wire. Perhaps only from this wire can you appreciate the quarry-but I'll never know! In the mid nineteenth century it was one of the largest in the world, employing 2,800 men. Waterfalls at Pont Ogwen provide an excuse to pause, for this track is steep in places, steep enough for wheel-spin in wet conditions. The drama in this Act is intense enough for sporadic spontaneous bursts of conviviality among the players.

Act Four begins at Pont y Ceunant, and begins slowly. Lôn Las Ogwen joins the old metalled road in Nant Ffrancon, which calmly and gently steers you into the big mountains, the Carneddau opposite, and ahead the Glyderau, Clogwyn-Du and Tryfan. It was along here at Christmas 1947 that a 17 year old Mancunian apprentice builder walked in steady drizzle, having arrived at Bangor Railway Station at 2 a.m.. For the next four days Joe Brown and his mates climbed all the routes on Idwal Slabs. It was sleeting and snowing, they were camping and they wore gym shoes. A year later they returned to find the Devil's Kitchen (Twll Du) cliffs 'fluted with an organ-pipe formation of

Porth Penrhyn

icicles' (Joe Brown The Hard Years). To the left of Hanging Garden Gully he described ' the lower hundred feet of this section was scooped into a great overhanging wall, with another hundred feet of vertical wall above. Draped down this was a cascade of ice-the top part attached to the rock, but the lower part hanging in space like a chandelier.'

Extras in the valley include sheep marked with a red heart. The final half mile climb to Idwal Cottage is steep, but there you'll find the new tea bar.

The play's sponsors were the Pennants. Richard Pennant, the First Baron Penrhyn, was a slave owner, MP and Irish peer, and married into the Penrhyn Estate. In the 1790s he bought out independent slate quarriers, appropriated Crown lands, built roads, tramways and the Porth Penrhyn harbour. On Richard's death, George Hay Dawkins-Pennant, his cousin, expanded the estate to 26,278 acres, and with the quarry at Bethesda producing 150,000 tons of finished slate a year, he became one of the wealthiest men in Britain. He built, in 1827-36 the magnificent neo-Norman Castell Penrhyn, also described as a 'vast,

Through the wooded Ogwen valley

grotesque monument'. George Sholto Gordon Douglas-Pennant took over in 1886, an old-school, hunting, shooting, fishing Tory, he hardly ever visited Gwynedd, but his authoritarianism and arrogance led to the terrible quarrymen's strike of 1900-1903. After years of dissatisfaction and unrest among the quarrymen, they clubbed together and formed a union, the NWQU. Lord Penrhyn was determined to break this unionisation and maintain his iron-fist control over his workers, so he locked them out, beginning one of the longest-lasting disputes in the industrial history of Britain. As in all disputes the pressure to feed their families and pay the rent led to terrible conflict within the community of Bethesda, and eventually the workers had to give in. At the time Lord Penrhyn had inherited the largest estate rental in England and Wales, also plantations in Jamaica and the Parliamentary seat of Caernarvonshire. His annual rent roll was around £67,000, and his income from the quarry about £150,000 per annum, equivalent to about £25 million today. So when you read the information boards around the estate, bear this in mind. Of course I'm biased, I come from a family of miners.

Other local cycle tracks

For a detailed guide to local cycle routes read Phil Horsley's *Cycle Guide to Snowdonia*, published by Gwasg Carreg Gwalch.

Sustrans NCN 5 leaves Lôn Las Ogwen near to Bangor and with a mix of on / off road goes east to Conwy and Llandudno to meet up with the previous trail in this book, *The North Coast Cycleway*.

In the other direction, also from Bangor, Lôn Las Menai takes the old railway line to Caernarfon, again to a large extent off road, and there it meets the next trail in this book, Lôn Eifion.

Snippets
The Holyhead Road

The Act of Union in 1800 which unified Great Britain and Ireland required the construction between the two capitals of the first major civilian state-funded road building programme since the Romans, the Holyhead Road. The road survives in many places, including Nant Ffrancon, though with many new layers of tarmac on top. Thomas Telford (see Trail 10 Llangollen Canal) was a natural choice as engineer, with the Pontcysyllte Aqueduct completed in 1805 and a growing reputation as a builder of bridges and roads. In Nant Ffrancon the old road, upon which you are cycling, built by Lord Penrhyn in 1792 to his new inn in Capel Curig, had the disadvantage of a steep twisting section up to Llyn Ogwen. For the swift passage of mail coaches to Dublin Telford required a maximum gradient of 1 in 20, sweeping curves and flattened bridges. Upon this road the 'Wonder' coach could cover over a hundred miles in a day.

Nant Ffrancon

13. Lôn Las Cefni

Newborough Forest through Llangefni to Cefni Reservoir

Distance: *17½ km / 10½ m*
OS Map: *1:50,000 114 Anglesey*
Leaflet: *Sustrans Lôn Las Cefni*
Anglesey Rural Cycling (Isle of Anglesey County Council)
Access and Parking:
Cefni Reservoir, near Rhosmeirch
Llangefni
Pentre Berw
Malltraeth
Newborough Forest
Surface: *Tarmac, hardcore in the forest*
Nearby places of interest:
Beaumaris
Newborough
Ynys Llanddwyn
Plas Newydd
Bryncelli Ddu chambered cairn
Anglesey Sea Zoo

Ynys Môn (Anglesey) is not an island to whip off its T-shirt and shout its name from the highest hill. True, coaches gather in the lee of the (not yet completed) walls of Beaumaris castle, and in the car park of a railway station. Children bury granddads in Red Wharf Bay and the north of the island waits to see whether its generators will be fuelled by wind, water, trees or plutonium, but mostly the island ticks along growing grass to feed to cows and sheep.

Lôn Las Cefni follows the rift which splits the island, from Cefni Reservoir, through the 'capital' and market town of Llangefni, along Cors Ddyga / Malltraeth Marshes, over the Cob at Malltraeth and into Newborough Forest. It is essentially flat, well paved apart from both ends, well signed apart from the bit in Newborough Forest, traffic-free apart from a short section on a quiet road and the negotiation of Llangefni, easily accessed and just a nice easy ride through a rural landscape.

Like so many of the trails in this book its origins lie with industry. The Cob at Malltraeth was begun in 1790, but a breach delayed completion until 1812. The date is important, for Britain had been at war with France for the best part of 20 years. In the middle of Malltraeth Marshes the river is bridged by Pont Marquis, named after

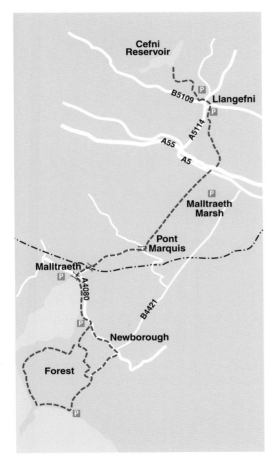

Henry Paget, the First Marquis of Anglesey. Lord Paget was an army officer and a politician. He was involved in the defeat by the French of the British in Flanders, returning to Britain and beginning an affair with Lady Charlotte, the Duke of Wellington's sister-in-law. So Wellington kept a beady eye on Paget, and was on hand to offer a complete lack of sympathy when Paget had his leg shattered following a spectacular cavalry charge at the Battle of Waterloo. The exchange is reported to have gone:

> Marquis of Anglesey (to Duke of Wellington) "My God, I've lost a leg."
> Duke of Wellington, in reply, "My God, so you have."

Paget was taken to the nearby home of Lady Hyacinthe where his leg was removed without antiseptic or anaesthetic. Paget then asked his lackey to take a look to make sure removal had been necessary, and was assured his leg was indeed beyond repair (and in any case, was now detached). Lady Hyacinthe subsequently turned her home into a shrine, with visitors, including the King of Prussia, being shown the bloody chair on which he had been seated, then the tombstone in the garden above the buried leg. Today we are not so mawkish, but the saw is on display at the National Army Museum, the revolutionary artificial leg (known as the 'Anglesey Leg') is on display in Plas Newydd, along with a trouser leg. I know not from which leg.

The Cob did four things. It enabled a road to be built from Newborough to Malltraeth; it made it easier for Telford's Holyhead Road to cross the marsh a little further inland; it enabled the fields to be improved to grow cereals; and it improved access to, and the drainage of, the coal mines along the edges of this valley. The Hollands opened the Pentre Berw colliery in 1815, with shafts 400 feet underground (the ruined surface buildings are still there). Mining ended in the 1880s with the closure of the Pont Marquis colliery, but the coal had been vital for industrial development locally and in particular for the smelters in Amlwch serving the huge copper mine on Parys Mountain.

Neglect and flooding led to the fields reverting to marsh, which is now managed by the RSPB with the prime aim of persuading bitterns to come and breed, and to manage the grassland for lapwing.

Also present are curlew, redshank, snipe and heron. The artist Charles Tunnicliffe moved to Malltraeth in 1947 to paint the local bird life.

Llangefni itself is not so conducive to the young or uncertain cyclist, but it is a short cross-town push over to the Dingle and a shared path and boardwalk run through the nature reserve to the reservoir Llyn Cefni.

At the other end, in Newborough Forest things can get a little sticky. The way-marked trail Lôn Las Cefni cuts through the forest to the service road closer to the village and Llys Rhosyr, one time manor of the Welsh Princes. Two other way-marked trails, Corsica and Bike Quest both lead to the main car park in the forest. These trails are easy to follow and flattish, though rough in places and paved with gravel and cockleshells. They run through the trees. Pop your head out now and then and survey the dunes, the small island of Ynys Llanddwyn and then across Bae Caernarfon to the peninsula of Llŷn and Arfon.

Lôn Las Cefni at Malltraeth

Snippets

Red squirrels. Anglesey is Wales' refuge for red squirrels. A programme for the eradication of greys is now complete and Anglesey declared in 2015 a grey squirrel-free zone. There are now 400/500 reds, some of whom live in Newborough Forest. Just 18 years ago the red squirrel population was close to extinction and the island swamped with over 3,000 greys. They were trapped and humanely killed and reds reintroduced and supported. The Sciurius Life Project, with EU funding, was launched in June 2016 with the aim of eradicating greys from much of Gwynedd.

Red squirrels live for 4-5 years but can fall prey to foxes, buzzards and cats, they can become road kill, suffer from malnutrition and recently have begun to suffer from the adenovirus. In humans this was recognised in World War 2 as being caused by conditions of crowding and stress. In Japan it is called 'pool fever' and in the USA 'boot camp flu'. The chief suspect on Anglesey in carrying the virus to squirrels is the humble wood mouse. It is a delicate thing, life.

Ynys Llanddwyn. Dwynwen, daughter of the King of Powys in the Fifth Century was, by all accounts, beautiful, and she fell for the swashbuckling Maelon. It didn't end well, with Maelon a block of ice, and in isolation Dwynwen offering herself to God on this island. She is the Welsh patron saint of lovers. The Abbey church was wrecked by Henry VIII; the two towers were built as lighthouses; and the pilots cottages now house a folk museum.

Newborough (*Niwbwrch*). As the name suggests, a new village, built here in 1303 to house the people of Beaumaris displaced when King Edward the First built his castle and garrison.

Newborough Forest. Planted after the War to save the village from wind-blown sand, and provide some employment, but now at risk from disease and the rising sea levels which could spell disaster for this coast. The plan is to improve diversity, though not many trees will withstand being planted into sand. The Management Plan also proposes to improve the recreation potential, hence the cycle trails, with the hope that one day the forest will have a tea bar. In reply to local opposition to the proposal to make Newborough Beach a nudist beach the Director of

Dingle, Llangefni

British Naturism is reported as saying, "What people forget is that naturists...come with money in their pockets."

Other local cycle trails

Lôn Las Cefni is the only off road cycle trail on Anglesey of any length, but the centre of the island is criss-crossed with quiet country lanes, many of which are unsullied with signposts. For more detailed information read Phil Horsley's *Cycle Guide to Anglesey*, published by Gwasg Carreg Gwalch.

Near Llyn Cefni

14. Lôn Eifion

Bryncir to Caernarfon

Distance: 20 km / 12½ m
OS Map: 1:50,000
115 Caernarfon and Bangor
123 Lleyn Peninsula
Leaflet: Gwynedd Recreational Routes
(Gwynedd Council)
Access and Parking:
Bryncir (easy to miss)
Penygroes
Inigo Jones Slate Works
Groeslon
Llanwnda
Caernarfon
Surface: Mainly tarmac with some
hardcore
Nearby places of interest:
Caernarfon
Glynllifon Country Park
Cricieth Castle
Lloyd George Museum,
Llanystumdwy

Lôn Eifion is popular. On it you'll meet granddads keeping the years at bay, fresh-faced lasses beaming with the joy of freedom, members of the Dwyfor Club fit, strong and enthusiastic, and dads in shorts fiddling with the tag-a-longs as infants chew their nails in trepidation. My job is to explain this popularity. It is not wildly romantic (as the Elan Valley), muscular (Lôn Las Ogwen), glamorous (Llangollen), erudite (Rheidol) or frivolous (North Coast Cycleway), but somehow when given the choice you make a date with Lôn Eifion. It is the boy-next-door of cycle paths.

Your best mate points out the flaws; the regular dismounts required to open gates; the lack of true breeding (the railway line was popularised by downtrodden Lancastrians heading for Butlins near Pwllheli); the occasional passages chaperoned by the A487; the incongruous beginning (round the back of the cattle market-easy to miss); the missing thrills (up over there are the snow clad eyries of Eryri, down there the baking golden sands of Bae Caernarfon, here we have the boggy grassland of Graianog.) There is no denying it ends well, delivering you to the foot of the Eagle Tower of Caernarfon Castle, and if you're very lucky

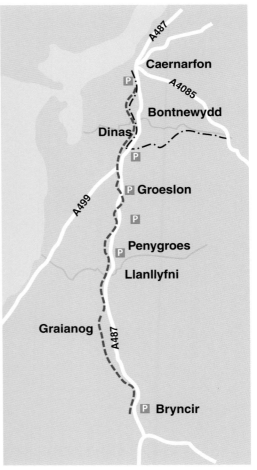

you'll be walked down the aisle by one of the six push-me-pull-you Garretts, ideal for the tortuous journey on the Welsh Highland Line.

So, if you will allow me, I'll be your personal guide:-

– Bryn Terfel grew up over there in Nantcyll-uchaf and behind is Mynydd Graig Goch, Red Rock Mountain, but only because hill-bagger Myrddyn Phillips re-calibrated its height in 2008 as six inches over the two thousand. Before that it was a hill. Of course, just like the life of a prize winning gooseberry, with rising sea levels, the situation is temporary.

– Where are we now? Graianog Crossing, middle of nowhere. The map shows plenty of prehistoric sites around here, Bronze Age, that's from around four and a half thousand years ago, including Burnt Mounds, probably used as cooking pits. Up ahead is the summit of the railway at just over five hundred feet elevation. Billy Butlin opened the Penychain holiday camp in 1947, with most people coming by train. In the mid 1950s daily holiday specials ran on this line from Euston, called the Welshman's Express, with up to 12 coaches, and double-headed.

– Over there is Penygroes. Nantlle Vale football club was once player-managed by Orig Williams, later to become the famous wrestler 'El Bandito'. He had a reputation as the man most often sent off in the Welsh League.

– And here on the left is The Wall. Inside is Glynllifon, a 102 roomed mansion rebuilt in the 1830s by Spencer Bulkeley Wynn, the Third Baron Newborough, and around it he built The Wall, ten kilometres long and up to four metres high. Why? Up the road at Faenol, Assheton Smith built a similar wall around his estate, within which he roamed a herd of temperamental cattle, deer and zebra. It also acted as a second barrier should any of the dangerous zoo animals escape. But that was fifty years later, and, if it wasn't built to keep things in, was it perhaps built to keep them out? The First Lord Newborough was well known for his 'military fantasies', and built Fort Belan on the coast as well as an armoury which he called Fort Williamsburg and around it the first wall, to repel either Napoleon or the Americans, or both. But by 1836 things were looking up, Napoleon was dead and the USA was looking south and west, life was good. Up to a point. The unrest began in Kent in 1830 under the mythical leadership of Captain Swing, and for a short while the whole countryside seemed on the verge of open rebellion against the daily grind of poverty, unemployment and dependency, marked by rick-burning, machine-breaking, arson and poaching. So it's my guess The Wall was built to keep out the great unwashed masses.

– Shall we finish on a lighter note? With the publication of 'Fire in my Blood' the tell-all story of the flame-haired siren Denisa Braun who married the Fifth Lord Newborough in 1939 despite being 28 to his 61, and despite an acquaintance telling her "Tommy Newborough doesn't want a wife, he wants a brood mare". Both had 'well-earned reputations'. Denisa failed to provide the longed-for son, but a daughter whom she named Blanche-neige. Thomas divorced her in 1947, having suffered the scousers of the 46th (Liverpool Welsh) Royal Tank Division training on and living in Glynllifon, and vacated the house in 1949 citing high taxation and the difficulty in obtaining servants.

– Here we are, lunch, the Welsh Rock Cafe at Inigo Jones Slate Works, with its musical heritage, including 'Tom Jones' knickers.

It is around this time, with ten miles already under your belt, and the rough grazing and shattered rock replaced by dripping trees, the sultry smell of gorse and glimpses of the sparkling sea, that thoughts come jumbling out; everyone you've met has spoken, from the best-dressed velos to the D.W. with the borzoi. It is such a pleasure being able to eat up the miles without worrying about a single car, one of those things-in-life-that-make-it-all-worthwhile, or as my Dad used to say when things were going particularly well, "It'll do"; and Lôn Eifion is so coherent, it's just lovely coming down from the grassy moor to the sea in one flow.

The trail ends a few car parks short of the walled town of Caernarfon. I take it for granted, it's the library, the cinema, it's where you change buses, but I shouldn't. If it were in the south of France it would be unbearably thronged. Add in the Garretts with their double powered bogies and it's easy to see why cyclists regularly return.

There is a potential fly in the ointment. A by-pass is scheduled for Caernarfon, departing from Llanwnda and crossing Lôn Eifion again somewhere to the west of Bontnewydd. There will be disruption during construction, but when it's done it should be fine, but there is the potential for more traffic interference, which would be a shame.

Snippets

The Mast. Erected in 1963 to bring ITV to Llŷn, it now transmits digitally, and at 1041 feet high, it is the tallest structure in Wales.

Dinas Station. Restored to its 1923 appearance, it is surrounded by the sheds of the Welsh Highland Railway, hence the rusting hulks awaiting restoration.

Llanllyfni. There existed in Llanllyfni a coeden bechod, a tree of sin. The family of a deceased would bake a cake or potato and leave it to cool on the chest of the departed, to absorb all their sins. This would then be placed under the coeden bechod, with a small amount of money and sometimes a glass of beer, to be consumed by the sin-eater and free the deceased to ascend to Heaven. It was the ultimate zero-hours contract being a sin-eater, plus they were avoided by the community and treated as lepers. It is said to continue today in Upper Bavaria and parts of Appalachia. The problem for sin-eaters, apart from the isolation and the unknown gap between meals, was that it was assumed that, over time, they absorbed a little of the sins of each soul they saved.

Other local cycle trails

Again, locally this is the only cycle trail of note apart from the ones already mentioned, and the short Lôn Las Menai which runs from Caernarfon to Bangor and is only partially off road. However Pen Llŷn offers some lovely cycling on quiet roads, although somewhat busier in the summer school holiday period. For more information read Phil Horsley's *Cycle Guide to Llŷn Peninsula*, published by Gwasg Carreg Gwalch.

15. Llwybr Mawddach Trail

Dolgellau to Barmouth (*Y Bermo*) and Fairbourne (*Y Friog*)

Distance: 13 km / 8 m
OS Map: 1:50,000
124 Porthmadog and Dolgellau
Leaflet: The Mawddach Trail
(Snowdonia National Park)
Access and Parking:
Dolgellau
Penmaenpool
Arthog
Morfa Mawddach
Barmouth
Fairbourne
Surface: Hardcore
Nearby places of interest:
Dolgellau
Coed y Brenin

And so we come to Llwybr Mawddach, the Mawddach Trail. It has been mentioned in dispatches and is nigh on perfect. Everyone using the trail has that air of the cat that found the cream. You even hear spontaneous whistling.

To the South Cadair Idris rises powerfully to almost 3000 feet. To the North your eye is drawn by the ruler-sharp walls to Diffwys (750 m / 2,500 ft), the last of the Rhinogydd, but it is to the estuary of Afon Mawddach to which the eye inevitably returns. At the eastern end the trail commences at Y Bont Fawr (*the large bridge*) in Dolgellau, and at the western end it terminates at the car park adjoining Morfa Mawddach Station, though you would be remiss to miss out on either of the extensions. Either cross Barmouth Bridge and cycle around through the town to the end of the Promenade, itself closed to motor vehicles on occasions as the sand slips silently into the town, like the Sahara, or the creepy Japanese film Woman of the Dunes; or bike along the flood embankment to visit Fairbourne (*Y Friog*) a village with the dubious honour of seeing house prices fall sharply in recent times. The SMP2 (Shoreline Management Plan 2) has suggested that the village could be under water in 100 years and would then be 'decommissioned'. Residents have responded by seeking £100 million

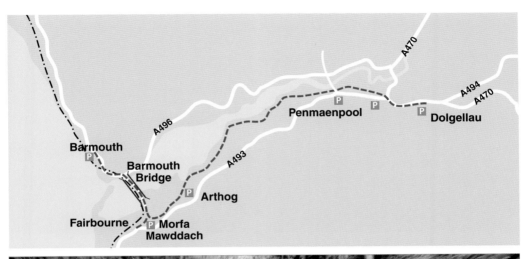

*1. Mawddach estuary; 2. A closer view
of the railway/cycling bridge*

compensation from somebody, or something. (And to think I began this description so positively and I'm already drowning in sand, sea and litigation.)

You are hot on the heels of great Victorians. Charles Darwin walked over the hills in 1828 to explore both locally and intellectually with fellow students in Barmouth. He also stayed in later life at Plas Caerdon across the estuary. The poets came here, escaping the 'sulky blotch', the 'blur of soot and smoke' (Dickens) spreading across industrial England. Shelley came with his then wife Harriet in 1812 (see the Elan Valley Trail for juicy gossip on Shelley), Wordsworth in 1824, Lord Byron too, following the glowing recommendation of Barmouth by Thomas Pennant. Later in the century Gladstone, William Wilberforce and General Booth (the founder of the Salvation Army) were regular visitors, as was John Ruskin. Ruskin was part of the reaction among decent folk to the horrors of life in industrial Britain. He sketched out the framework of his own idea of utopia, in which art and life would merge, work would be by hand without polluting machinery and interspersed with folk festivals. No wonder he favoured Barmouth, hardly a factory to behold, and festivals galore, according to the boards in the railway station, including country music, line dancing and running up mountains. In 1871 Ruskin founded the Guild of St George and Mrs Fanny Talbot donated 13 cottages on the hill in Barmouth for 'the well being and happiness of working men and to prevent them from slipping into beggary and poverty.' Ruskin was more of an ideas man than hands-on and some of his other schemes slipped from 'would-be garden of Eden' to 'a scene of confusion' (Totley Colony in Sheffield) and he reputedly was put off carnal relations with his wife Effie when she failed to resemble a Greek statue on their wedding night.

The Cambrian Railway, from Machynlleth, was responsible for Barmouth Bridge in 1867. The Great Western Railway completed the line upon which you ride, from Ruabon (see Trail 10), through Dolgellau to Barmouth a year later, bringing tourists and taking away slate and the thick, white cloth made in Dolgellau and known as Webbs or Welsh Plains, much of which was shipped to North America and used for covered wagons. At Fegla Fawr the Cardiff bus magnate, Soloman Andrews, built a family resort, commandeered by the Royal Marines in preparation for the D-Day Landings. Fairbourne was constructed by Mr Arthur McDougal (of the flour) using bricks from his nearby brick-works. Beneath the modern conservatories, extensions and towers, the modest brick bungalows can still be seen.

Under threat of closure is the cyclist and pedestrian path on Barmouth bridge, the cash-strapped Gwynedd Council finding it difficult to find the annual £30,800 paid to Network Rail for the right of way.

Such is the idyllic nature of the trail that Annie says, "Why doesn't everyone ride a bike?" At the very height of summer it can sometimes feel as if they do, and Dolgellau turns into a Welsh Amsterdam.

The trail is maintained by the National Park not just for cyclists, who are reminded to be courteous towards other users on horseback and in wheelchair.

Annie has the habit of saying, "Dring Dring" when approaching people from behind. It was suggested, somewhere near the RSPB Observatory, by a lady in pink trousers with an unruly poodle, that this really should be "Ding-a-ling". Ding-a-ling!

When we talked to him last the RSPB chap was still smarting from the refusal of planning permission for the construction of a platform in the channel for the sole use of ospreys, on the grounds that Life should not be too Perfect. But should an osprey turn up out of the blue, and by the strangest chance find the perfect, ready-made platform already there...

At this stage, with Fairbourne and Barmouth under threat from rising sea levels, Dolgellau sometimes threatened by damaging flooding, and the surrounding woodland trees in danger from both disease and climatic extremes, let me briefly mention global warming.

Actually there are two global warmings. There is the slow steady and undeniable heating of the planet, with records broken each year. We don't really feel this as our changeable weather dominates and Wales is situated in an area of the world which will be less affected by extremes. Other parts are already suffering droughts and water shortages. Also we are talking about measuring the planetary heating on land. There is a delaying effect, with the cooler oceans warming more slowly, estimated at perhaps 25 years. We are warming the planet and even if we stop now it will continue to heat up.

Then there is the other global warming. News of this one may have reached our brains, but it has not yet set off the red flashing lightbulbs nor activated the sirens. In order to stabilise global warming and reverse the heating trend we not only have to stop pumping out greenhouse gases, we also have to begin to extract them from the atmosphere. We know of two ways to do this, the first is unproven technology, the second is the planting of trees, which consume CO_2 and give us oxygen, and in order to plant enough trees it is suggested that we must change out diet. We do still have a choice.

Other local cycle trails

Not far away are two other cycle trails, one off road, the other virtually so. Llwybr Llyn Traws Lake Path is a new cycle path which circumnavigates Llyn Trawsfynydd, 13 km / 8 m in length. Lon Dysynni is an easy on

Crossing the bridge at Penmaenpool

road path from Tywyn through lush countryside and fairly traffic free. For more details see the Snowdonia Cycle Guide.

Snippets
The Quakers of Dolgellau

In 1657 George Fox visited Dolgellau and, looking down on the valley of Afon Wnion, declared he had found paradise on earth. He gathered a devoted band of worshippers in the valley, including Rowland Ellis of Bryn Mawr, who, when the persecution became too great, led many of them to emigrate to Pennsylvania in 1686. In 2014 the children of Ysgil Y. Gader collectively wrote the Book of Sufferings about the local Quakers, reflecting the Meeting for Sufferings which dates back to the 17th Century to record and help the sufferings of Quakers. These days it has more of a communications role in the Society of Friends.

George Fox took the words of James in the Bible and refused to swear by the name of the Lord to tell the truth in Court, for which he was imprisoned many times. His words were sung by Jimmy Cliff in 1968;

And let your yeah be yeah
And your no be no, now.

16. Rheidol Cycle Trail / Llwybr Beicio Rheidol

Aberystwyth to Cwm Rheidol / Devil's Bridge (*Pontarfynach*)

Distance: *17 km / 11 m*
OS Map: *1:50,000*
135 Aberystwyth and Machynlleth
Leaflet: *Available from Tourist Information*
Access and Parking:
Aberystwyth
Cwm Rheidol
Canolfan Ymwelwyr Visitor Centre
Rheidol Power Station
Rheidol Mines
Surface: *Mainly on-road, with tarmac'd paths to begin with*
Nearby places of interest:
Aberystwyth
– Ceredigion Museum, situated in the restored Edwardian theatre, the Coliseum.
– Pier and Pavilion. Special mention for the roosting starlings.
– Constitution Hill. Camera Obscura and Cliff Railway.
– National Library of Wales, including exhibitions in Gregynog Gallery.
Cwm Rheidol. Magic of Life Butterfly House.
Ponterwyd. The Llywernog silver/lead mine is a museum

Let us not be too hasty about jumping in the saddle to begin this voyage from Aber to Cwm Rheidol. We can warm up with a game of crazy golf ('A great round of crazy golf', 4* on Tripadvisor). Crazy golf was patented as Golfstacle in 1907 but did not arrive in Aber until after the last war, and is located below the castle grounds (Norman, rebuilt by Edward Longshanks, captured by Owain Glyndŵr, destroyed by Cromwell). From the castle we can enjoy a vista of the promenade, devastated by the storms in the winter of 2012/13 and not as popular with the motor-biking fraternity as it used to be due to the enforcement of parking charges.

Aber has been described as an island of

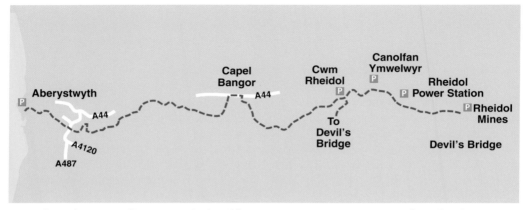

enforced cosmopolitanism. It is the oldest health resort on the west Welsh coast with a climate 'sunny, dry and bracing'. The railways arrived in the 1860s bringing 'health and pleasure seekers'. On the front Thomas Savin built a superior hotel to profit from the in-comers, an immediate failure, but the hotel was soon equipped with three professors and twenty six students and opened as University College. In 1896 King Edward the Seventh (then Prince of Wales) was installed as Chancellor, and a degree of Doctor of Music bestowed on his long-suffering (see Trail 11) wife Queen Alexandra. The University has since infiltrated the town

creating 'an array of subcultures', including film stars and dogs named Aristotle and Mephistopheles.

Enough, let us mount, beginning at the Lifeboat Station and passing under Trefechan Bridge (designed by Szlumper, more anon.) with its plaque telling us about an early protest (1963) against the mistreatment of the Welsh language. Signage is a little shaky and the cycle path in town is popular so, keeping Afon Rheidol on your right, pass Morrisons and the rugby ground, cross the river, pass the cricket ground and a wood and you're at the sewage works (where else?). The next stretch is through an industrial estate, which comes as both a shock and an affront, partly on shared footpaths, partly on roads. Clarity and coherence take a back seat. Basically take a right at Wynnstay and a left at Glanrafon and you're on a country lane, which I am assured is mostly very quiet apart from the daily milk tanker and occasional frenzied bursts of sludge tankers.

The trail is a little like crazy golf, mostly easy-peasy with obstacles now and then to overcome. One such is Capel Bangor where the cycle path has commandeered the footpaths for 400 yards alongside the A44.

If you're lucky you'll witness a Battle of Britain encounter between the red kites and a mob of crows.

The railway is, of course, the Vale of Rheidol line. The Szlumpers (James Weeks Szlumper, Alfred Weeks, Albert Weeks, William Weeks) were a railway family. Their father, a Polish émigré tailor escaping the forthcoming brave but calamitous war with Tzar Nicholas' Russia, somehow ended up in Pembrokeshire. James Weeks Szlumper (the engineer you've never heard of) became Surveyor to the County of Cardiganshire, but his main interest was railways. Now west Wales is not easy terrain for railwaymen, but two of Szlumper's survive, the Welsh Highland Railway (see Trail 14) and the Vale of Rheidol. This was built by Irish navvies laid off after the completion of the Elan Valley reservoirs (see Trail 8), and opened in 1902, just in time for the transportation of worshippers to the isolated chapels in the valley during the 1904-06 religious revival fervour. In the forecourt of Penllwyn Chapel in Capel Bangor is a bust by the sculptor Sir Goscombe John of Dr Lewis Edwards, the founder of the Calvinistic Methodist College in Bala. Also born here was John Roberts (Ieuan Gwyllt), a pioneer of congregational hymn singing. I should point out that in Wales, the 'English' surname is derived from an ancestral patronymic (John the son of Robert) and the Welsh name from the place of origin (here the assumed Bardic name, Ieuan of the Wild Wood).

The valley of Cwm Rheidol intrigues as it narrows into a 'V', with steep sided

1. The old College; 2. Ceredigion museum; 3. Aberystwyth beach and promenade

slopes and just a poop-poop now and then of steam. It is unusual these days to see deciduous woodland on both valley sides (Welsh [sessile] oak, wych elm, small-leafed lime). I am describing here only the valley route. The main Rheidol Trail to Devil's Bridge involves a long, steep climb out of the valley and a mile or so of 'A' road, itself not particularly conducive to safe cycling. At Devil's Bridge is the Hafod Hotel, featured in Hinterland (see previously mentioned 'film stars') built as a Swiss style chateau with a tea room and a bar. George Borrow, in 1854, described the 'monk's boiling cauldron, the long, savage, shadowy cleft, and the grey, crumbling, spectral bridge'. The three stacked bridges and the Punchbowl have attracted visitors to Devil's Bridge ever since, many coming by train.

Staying in the valley, the road narrows beyond the Cwmrheidol hydroelectric power scheme, (silently producing power since 1961, cafe, guided tours), and is dotted with chapels, new extensions in corrugated iron and a greenhouse in the shape of a caboose. The trail ends at the

1. The Llywernog silver/lead mine;
2. Devil's Bridge

huge mine workings, the tailings slowly being covered with trees. A meadow runs down to the lovely river.

The elephant in the room (or canary in the cage) is lead mining. Lead miners and chapel-goers are not among us in huge numbers these days so it is not easy to appreciate their lives. Mining still holds a fascination, for who can imagine working underground in cramped, hot and dangerous conditions. Lead mining did (and does, for it must continue somewhere) not have the combustible air which led to my Grandfather being fatally burned underground in a coal mine in the 1930s, but it was said that by the time a man got to be a good miner he was physically past it (average life expectancy of 32). The main problems were:

– carbon monoxide poisoning. As men and candles used up the oxygen underground the air became 'bad', known as "the damps".

– lead poisoning. 'Blue gum' was a sign that things weren't well. I won't go into details on the effects on the human body.

– lung disease (silicosis), caused by dust breathed underground, released into the air by drilling. As a boy I watched The

Lone Ranger in the house next door while in the bedroom above Henry was dying from silicosis. The effects have been described as 'The men appear thoroughly worn out and decrepit, even in their thirties.'

– accidents. Falling rock; falling down shafts; water bursts and flash flooding; gunpowder blasting.

Children worked underground until the mid-1800s (they were sent up the flues to clean off the lead which had settled on the sides). Thankfully the Mines Act of 1842 prohibited all girls and boys under ten years of age from working underground. The miners lived in tiny unhealthy cottages, for which they paid rent, or in mine barracks, described as 'dirty, disordered and uncomfortable places, where men slept two to a bed'.

Ystumtuen Mine (known as Cwm Rheidol) was worked constantly from 1750 to 1917, with an aerial rope-way carrying the ore and metals to the railway, though the consequences continue today. Mercasite (iron sulphide) sometimes occurred as metre-thick ribs. It was extracted and sold for the manufacture of sulphuric acid. Today, deep underground, the acid releases harmful metals, zinc, lead and cadmium into the drainage. The CEGB settling tank of the 1970s stopped working effectively some time ago so the pollution of the river ran right down to the sea. An experimental filtration plant was installed in 2011. The problem is exacerbated by the non-maintenance of the C19th drainage tunnels. In the late 1960s a blocked adit was disturbed resulting in 500,000 gallons of ocherous acidic water flowing into Afon Rheidol, killing thousands of fish.

People have opinions, which they share, Jim Perrin on wind-farms, George Monbiot on sheep, Annie on red kite feeding stations, my mate Tony on agricultural subsidies. We live in a skewed, oppressive, all-action world under the flailing heavy hand of man, but for a while, on a bicycle you can breathe, clear your head, forget about your troubles and the troubles of the world, and just enjoy living.

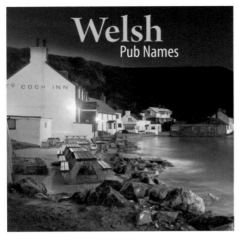

COMPACT CYMRU
– MORE TITLES;
128 PAGES
£5.95
FULL OF COLOUR IMAGES
AND CONCISE WRITING

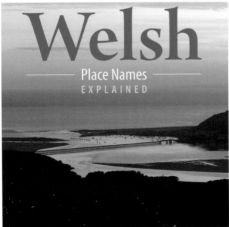

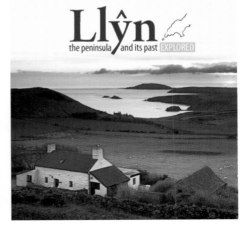

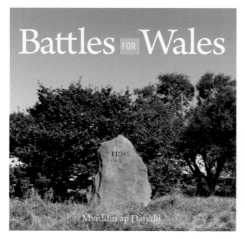

Battles FOR Wales

1136

Myrddin ap Dafydd

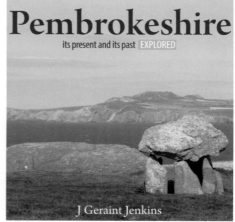

Pembrokeshire
its present and its past EXPLORED

J Geraint Jenkins

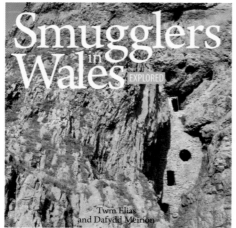

Smugglers in Wales EXPLORED

Twm Elias
and Dafydd Meirion

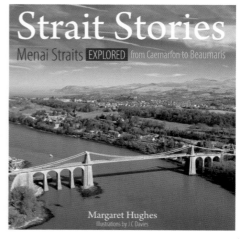

Strait Stories
Menai Straits EXPLORED from Caernarfon to Beaumaris

Margaret Hughes
Illustrations by J C Davies